Paul,

With love and bes

us all

XXX

11th December 1992.

MORE THAN A MATCH

A Player's Story

LEE CHAPMAN

STANLEY PAUL

LONDON

Stanley Paul & Co. Ltd
An imprint of Random House UK Ltd
20 Vauxhall Bridge Road, London SW1V 2SA

Random House Australia Pty Ltd
20 Alfred Street, Milsons Point, Sydney, NSW 2061

Random House New Zealand Ltd
18 Poland Road, PO Box 40–086, Glenfield, Auckland 10

Random House South Africa Pty Ltd
PO Box 337, Bergvlei 2012, South Africa

First published 1992

Set in Linotron Sabon by
Falcon Graphic Art Ltd, Wallington, Surrey

Printed and bound in Great Britain by
Clays Ltd, St Ives PLC

A catalogue record for this book is available
upon request from the British Library

ISBN 0 09 177502 7

Photographic Acknowledgments
The author and publishers would like to thank the
following for allowing use of copyright photographs:
Action Images, AllSport, Colorsport, Andrew Varley

Contents

· 1 ·

Operation Championship

A Football League championship winner's medal was the last thing on my mind as I lay in the operating theatre at Leeds General Infirmary in the late hours of 15 January 1992.

An hour earlier, in the dying stages of Leeds United's FA Cup tie against Manchester United, I had fallen heavily on my left hand after challenging with Gary Pallister for a cross by Mel Sterland. Defeat always hurts – and minutes later the final whistle sounded on a 1–0 victory for Manchester United – but seldom as much as this.

As the ball approached me, I felt certain I was about to score the equalising goal. Such was my concentration, I could only focus on the ball and was totally unaware of Pallister as he backed into me and knocked me off balance, just before I made contact. The collision had the double effect of forcing my header wide of the goal and knocking me to the ground. In my eyes a penalty should have been given, but the referee judged it to be a fair challenge.

In an attempt to break the fall, my left arm had taken my full weight of nearly fourteen stone. As I picked myself up, I felt a searing pain above my wrist. I looked down and saw my lower arm grotesquely out of shape, with a huge lump protruding from its upper surface. I knew instantly it was broken.

Alan Sutton, our physiotherapist, ran on to the pitch and attempted to examine my arm. 'Don't touch it!' I screamed. 'It's fucking broken! Just get me to hospital.' I was genuinely afraid that any movement would cause the broken bone to sever an artery.

Then, amidst all the confusion, came a pure comic moment. Alan instinctively reached for his 'magic' sponge and attempted to bathe my arm in cold water. It really would have had to be magic for it to have any effect. 'It's fucking broken,' I repeated. Alan stopped in his tracks and escorted me off the pitch. I remember walking past the dugouts, grimacing in agony, and receiving a pat on the back from the Manchester United manager, Alex Ferguson.

If I had thought the initial pain was severe then it paled into insignificance compared to the suffering I was to endure for the next thirty minutes. Once inside the treatment room, I was placed on a table to be examined by the club doctors. As my adrenalin level subsided, the intensity of the pain increased until it reached a level where I was unable to control myself. It was the worst I have experienced and was not helped by that fact that the ambulance, and with it the painkilling injection I so desperately needed, took twenty minutes to arrive.

One of the doctors briefly attempted to pull off my wedding ring and in doing so caused a knife-like pain on the underside of my wrist. I discovered later it was the broken bone of my ulna which had almost pierced the skin.

Once in the ambulance I at last received a painkilling injection, which took ten minutes to take full effect. Meanwhile, every little bump in the road sent fresh bolts of pain shooting down my arm.

Fortunately for me, the orthopaedic surgeon at the Infirmary, John Lawton, is a keen Leeds fan and had been present at the game. He had been alerted and was there to meet me when the ambulance arrived. Within the hour I was being wheeled to the operating theatre, without a care in the world after my 'pre-med' jab. Even the knowledge that I had suffered a Colles' fracture (the fracture of both the radius and the ulna) did not seem to worry me.

My wrist was broken, and so was the Leeds dream of the championship, according to many, pundits and public alike. Admittedly we were still top of the First Division, having won 6–1 at Sheffield Wednesday four days earlier, but Manchester United had matches in hand, plus the kind of strength to cover for injuries such as my own. More than that, they had now established what many people outside the Leeds dressing room considered to be a massive psychological advantage over us.

Three times in a fortnight, around the halfway stage of the season, we had enjoyed the home advantage against Alex Ferguson's team – in the League, Rumbelows Cup and FA Cup – and three times we had failed to beat them. The best we could manage was a 1–1 draw from the first game in the series, followed by 3–1 and

1–0 defeats, while they had beaten us at home and away in the Rumbelows semi-final a year previously.

We urgently needed to get back to winning ways on the Saturday, when Crystal Palace, the only side to have beaten us in the League up to that point, were due at Elland Road. Unfortunately, I would not be there to help against our other bogey team. My wrist was set in plaster and I was told by Mr Lawton, the surgeon, that I should not play for at least eight weeks, or even resume training for a month. I was at a low ebb – all the more so when I learned that certain Manchester United players had been gloating over my injury in the players' bar after our third meeting – and so were the team, it seemed, who stumbled to a 1–1 draw against Palace without me.

Yet a little more than three months later, after another heady Sunday in Sheffield – this time at Bramall Lane, home of United – we clinched the title. Our success seemed to surprise everyone, from the stunned supporters of Manchester United to our own manager, Howard Wilkinson, who was lost for words when ITV's Elton Welsby asked him if the achievement had 'sunk in'. I do not think it had, nor had it for any of the players. Howard is a manager whose strength has been in his thorough preparation, and long-term strategy. While he will have planned to win the game's top honour eventually, I think he was genuinely surprised to win it so soon. It may have seemed to him, as it did to me, after so many years competing for it without success, that the championship was a prize destined to be won by others.

Howard had taken over the manager's job from Billy Bremner, one of seven successors to Don Revie, on 10 October 1988. He had taken control early in the season, when Leeds were twenty-first in the Second Division. Not only was relegation avoided, but the Second Division championship was attained in his first full season. I was to join them in the January of that campaign, and scored the goal at Bournemouth that took Leeds back into the big time once again, after a period of eight years in the wilderness.

The club's return to the First Division proved to be successful for us both. In a season that saw us finishing an impressive fourth, I had the great satisfaction of scoring a total of thirty-one goals to finish as the division's top scorer.

The build-up to the 1991-92 season was full of optimism at Leeds, as it is at most clubs. Our squad was given an injection of much-needed pace with the acquisition of Tony Dorigo from Chelsea for £1.3 million, Rod Wallace from Southampton for £1.6 million and Steve Hodge from Nottingham Forest for £900,000. Another, seemingly minor, signing at that time was Jon Newsome from Sheffield Wednesday for the relatively modest fee of £140,000. No one could have foreseen the drama he would be involved in nine months later.

The squad underwent the usual six weeks of intensive training. A week-long tour of Ireland was followed by a trip to Tokyo to play the Brazilian side, Botafogo, at the Tokyo Dome in front of 41,000 fans.

Things were not going entirely smoothly, however. Mel Sterland and Tony Dorigo had undergone hernia operations and were struggling to make the start of the season. Another worry was Steve Hodge who was unable to take part in training, a problem he had come to expect – it was his seventh consecutive absence from pre-season training, all of them caused by unfortunate injuries.

The first game of a new season is always eagerly anticipated, the absence of competitive action for almost three months creating great enthusiasm amongst both players and supporters. We spent our final week of pre-season training in preparation for our first game, at Crystal Palace. Palace always pose problems from set-piece plays, and with this in mind, we had spent many hours on the training ground in rehearsal – only to be told on the Thursday that the game had been postponed because of uncompleted building work at Selhurst Park. It was a severe disappointment, and the feeling of anticlimax was intense. It seemed that all our hard work had been in vain. A hastily arranged match against Aldershot on the Friday night was hardly the way for a championship campaign to open. Ironically, our opponents that evening would be out of existence by the time we put the finishing touches to our season.

Our first taste of real action came the following Tuesday, at home to Nottingham Forest. Tony Dorigo had not quite made it in time, and his replacement at full back was John McClelland, a sprightly thirty-five-year-old. A much-needed winning start, thanks to a Gary McAllister goal, was the reward for a hard-working display. Our successful opening to the season was marred, however, by a knee injury to Chris Fairclough. Sustained at Southampton in our third match, it was to keep him out for five weeks. This was counteracted by the return of Mel Sterland in the following match against Manchester United at Old Trafford. John McClelland was switched to centre half, proving his adaptability.

We were certainly aware that our encounter with United was important, but we could not have predicted the extent of our rivalry over the coming months. United had stormed to the top of the table and had not conceded a goal in four matches. The League table had a familiar look about it, with Liverpool trailing by a single point.

The game was played in a searing heat that was hardly conducive to energetic football. Towards the end of the first half, Gary Speed received the ball in space on the left flank. He exploited that space, and sent over a vicious, swerving cross to the far post. It travelled into the area that keepers hate – eight yards out and between centre half and the goal. Peter Schmeichel attempted to intercept, but was beaten by the pace and movement, allowing me to nip in behind Pallister and head into an open goal – 1–0. I am generally a slow starter and after three fruitless outings, I was delighted to get off the mark. United mounted a late second-half onslaught, instigated entirely by their inspirational captain Bryan Robson. It was he who in fact scrambled a loose ball over the line for an equaliser with only four minutes remaining. We were desperately disappointed to concede such a late goal, but heartened by our display against the team who were being strongly fancied by many experts.

A midweek home game against champions Arsenal followed. After an indifferent start, Arsenal gave their best performance to date in a display unequalled all season by any visitors to Elland Road. Early into the second half we were trailing 2–0. It was then we showed qualities we had lacked the previous season. Our increased resilience, no doubt aided by the influx of quality players, enabled us to fight back and salvage a point.

Things were definitely improving when, in the following home game, David Batty scored in a 3–0 win over Manchester City, against whom his only other strike had come 160 games and almost four years earlier. The fact had been a constant source of ribbing for David from both the manager and the players. A down side to this win was the loss of Rod Wallace for seven matches with a hamstring injury. Another unwanted record was soon broken when Leeds gained their first victory over Liverpool since the Revie era, eighteen years earlier. This win, secured by a Steve Hodge goal, convinced us more than any other that we could compete successfully against the best.

Although we had enjoyed a ten-match unbeaten start, we trailed Manchester United by six points. Those were early days, though, and everybody knew it. What was more significant was our unfortunate run of injuries to Fairclough, Sterland and Wallace. Much had been made of Manchester United's superior squad strength and how important this would prove to be. On paper we were in no position to argue, but it did seem that outsiders were perhaps underestimating our reserve strength. It had already been severely tested and not been found wanting.

The following game, the rearranged fixture at Crystal Palace, brought our first defeat of the season. We conceded a sloppy injury-time goal from a hotly disputed free kick. It was a lesson in concentration for us: such was our annoyance with the referee, we allowed our guard to drop and were severely punished.

During the rest of October, we bounced back and enjoyed three consecutive victories, culminating in a home win against Oldham, another of our bogey teams. We had suffered a terrible record against Joe Royle's side over the past few years, but this victory enabled us to go top of the First Division for the first time since Leeds won the League in 1974. Our main aim at this point was to remain in the top two. In fact we had set our sights on never being out of it since we attained second place in mid-September. However, there still was not a real belief that we could maintain this lofty position – not yet anyway.

The game against Oldham was won by virtue of an own goal by Brian Kilcline, who ironically had been brought back into the side specifically to mark me. If Manchester United cringed at the sight of this blunder, it was nothing to what was in store in the penultimate round of fixtures in April – it was indeed an omen of things to come.

The period following the Oldham game was memorable for some stunning away performances which made people really sit up and take Leeds seriously. Our televised 4–1 victory at Aston Villa gave notice to anybody who held any doubts. It was an awesome display of powerful, attractive football which won many admirers. Mel Sterland and Gordon Strachan were the chief tormentors as the Villa defence was bombarded with devastating crosses from the right flank. Rod Wallace had previously been unable to settle due to injury. Now, on his return, he was starting to blossom and ignoring the inhibiting factor of his large fee. The Villa victory was notable in that it confirmed our belief in our ability. This was enhanced shortly afterwards by a repeat performance, and identical scoreline, at Everton in the Rumbelows Cup.

While we were enjoying great success away from home, it was becoming increasingly difficult to win at Elland Road. Teams were viewing their visits with some trepidation and were arriving with a very defensive attitude. Not only were opponents happy to leave with a draw, but as Peter Shreeves, the Spurs manager, admitted, they were also being turned on by the electric atmosphere generated by our supporters. Our third successive home draw came against Manchester United at the end of December. It was the first in a trilogy of home matches against them in the League, the Rumbelows Cup and the FA Cup. Many people were regarding the outcome of these games as significant in deciding the eventual title winners.

The match was fiercely contested, with United possibly shading the first half. They took an early lead in the second half which signalled a typical Leeds fightback. We were eventually awarded a late penalty, converted by Mel Sterland, which was enough to give us a share of the points. United certainly looked a solid, well-organised outfit and we knew they were going to be there or thereabouts at the end of the season. Our critics were saying they had more flair and improvisation than us, qualities which would see them through. The draw enabled them to remain top by two points; more importantly, they had two games in hand. We knew they were in pole position, but we were also aware that a lot could happen before the season was over.

Sandwiched between the two Manchester United Cup ties was our game at Sheffield Wednesday. Again, it was televised live, something that seemed to bring out the best in us. We did not disappoint and gave a performance that I consider to be our finest display of free-flowing football; this is the game I would like to be shown as an example of how well we can play. The 6–1 victory was Wednesday's record home defeat. The fact that England's Chris Woods was in goal for them only emphasised the heights we attained that afternoon.

It was a great personal triumph for me as I scored a hat trick against my former club. Hillsborough holds many fond memories for me, but this was a feat that I had never achieved during my time there. It was also the first hat trick on opposition soil by a Leeds player for more than twelve years.

Much had been made of our supposed weakness in terms of

squad strength and of how we could not perform without key members of the team. With this in mind our performance was even more impressive, since we were without Gordon Strachan through injury and David Batty through suspension. Carl Shutt and Steve Hodge came in to prove what vital members of the squad they were, combining with Mel Sterland, Tony Dorigo and Gary Speed to tear Wednesday apart down both flanks. I received the finest service I had had during my time at Leeds.

The game even had its comic moment, when a scantily clad woman ran on to the pitch. The lady turned out to be the owner of a massage parlour who was protesting at a decision to tax her earnings. No one, it seems, can escape the clutches of the Inland Revenue. After prolonged inaction by everyone at the ground, it was left to me to ask her to leave the pitch. My action attracted great publicity the following day. It was even unfairly suggested that I was asking for her phone number. . . .

The reaction to our win in the dressing room afterwards was the most ecstatic all season. The manager even leapt on to the treatment table in a show of jubilation. There were many reasons for our elation – the presence of the television cameras and the fact that the manager, myself, Mel Sterland and Carl Shutt had all played for Wednesday were just two – but the overriding one was that it was just one hell of a performance.

The two Cup ties against Manchester United were played on either side of the game at Wednesday. The first, in the Rumbelows Cup, had been a great disappointment to us all. We were soundly beaten 3–1 by a United team who were highly motivated after suffering a humiliating home defeat by QPR in their previous game. This kind of setback can, if the team possesses the right character, be a stimulus for future performances. United proved the point against us and we did the same at Wednesday. Every professional is aware that when the best teams are played directly after they have suffered a heavy defeat, there is nearly always a backlash with which to contend.

The fact that United had been obviously superior was hard to accept, although accept it we had to. Our most immediate route to Wembley had been blocked in a comprehensive manner, and I had tasted the humbling experience of being substituted. It was one I did not want to become accustomed to.

As our third meeting with United approached, we were all very much aware of the need for a convincing display. The balance of power had tilted in our rivals' favour and we knew it had to be redressed. We proceeded to give a powerful display, with Peter Schmeichel's goal leading a charmed existence. Time after time we found ourselves thwarted with goal-line chances, good saves and near misses. When my injury occurred, and the referee refused to give a penalty for the Pallister challenge, it was clear we were destined not to score. United undeservedly came away with a 1–0 victory.

Although we had lost we knew we had been the better team on the night and that overall there was not much to choose between the two sides. Any psychological damage to our championship campaign had been minimised by this last performance, and by the knowledge that by virtue of beating us United had let themselves in for several more games than we would now have to face. In fact, we wished them continued success in the Cup competitions as this would result in the type of backlog of fixtures we had experienced the season before. Our Cup success then had caused such a pile-up of games that we had to play four in seven days – a daunting prospect for any team. At the time, United's victories were being hailed as a turning point in the race for the title. They were – but not in the way the pundits thought. United's success at this stage was later to play a major part in their downfall, as the extra games finally caught up with them mentally and physically.

I knew only too well that my rehabilitation would be a period fraught with feelings of frustration at my inactivity and helplessness as I watched my team-mates play without me. What was even more annoying was that at the time of my injury, I had been playing as well as I had ever played. But then football often has a habit of knocking you down, just when things are going well. To be suddenly taken out of the first-team environment is a strange and uncomfortable experience. After being involved for so long, it is inevitable that a player in this situation is going to feel left out of things – and that's just what happened to me. Although I had suffered many injuries – numerous broken noses and fingers, to name a few – this was the most serious I had ever received and would necessitate my lengthiest spell out of the game. This inevitably fuelled speculation as to whether the manager would be prompted to open his cheque book and purchase a replacement. I knew the answer would lie in the team's results – a run of defeats would have demanded action, but I had faith in the existing squad to improvise until my return. Many names were bandied about, but I had suffered that problem ever since my arrival and was not unduly worried. In the eyes of the press, I had long been regarded as somewhat unfashionable, and even my goal ratio, which was better than a goal every two games, could not change this image. Many were also questioning the wisdom of not having a ready replacement, but the manager knew only too well I rarely missed matches.

The first game without me was against Crystal Palace. Howard Wilkinson experimented with Gary Speed at centre forward in an attempt to keep the team shape roughly the same. Palace, with their unattractive long-ball game, are always difficult to play against, as they attempt to wear the opposition down with their constant aerial bombardment. They proved so in this case and the game was drawn 1–1.

By the end of January we had regained the top position on goal difference, although United had one game in hand. The following game against Notts County enabled us to confirm our position with a 3–0 home victory. The manager then moved into the transfer market with the loan signing of Eric Cantona from the French club, Nîmes. I was aware of Eric from my time in France with Niort. At the time he had been banned from international football for a derisive outburst against the French national team manager. Now he was in more trouble for allegedly throwing a ball at a referee. We awaited his arrival with much interest and wondered how he would find life in English football. The manager was also reserving judgement, postponing a decision on a permanent move until the end of the season.

Time for me was passing painfully slowly. In an attempt to keep busy I was getting involved in as many activities as possible. A four-day holiday in Venice was followed by work for ITV on *The Match*. I was also commissioned by the *Sun* newspaper to report on the France-England rugby international in Paris. It was my first time at such a game and provided one of many valuable distractions during my tedious recovery period.

The one fortunate aspect of my injury was that I could not have chosen a better time to have almost seven weeks off. The other positive side-effect of our elimination from the two Cup competitions meant that I did not miss too many games, due to two free Cup weekends. I was in fact to miss a total of five. At almost any other period this figure would have been doubled.

As February drew to a close the urge to start playing again

became stronger and stronger. My cast had been removed and I was now involved in full training once again. I had set my sights on a comeback game against Luton Town on the 29th, but shortly before the match at Everton, the week before, I was asked by the manager if I thought I could play. It was a tempting question and one I may have answered differently a year previously. Then, after the horrendous facial injury I sustained at Spurs, I had played before I was ready. I had learned from that experience and was not going to make the same mistake twice – I would leave it another week. I was not going to let my desire to play cloud my judgement over my injury, although I know of many cases where this has happened, both with myself and with others.

Shortly before the Luton game, striker Tony Agana was signed on loan from Notts County. This was the match I had been aiming to play in, but as the game approached, reawakening memories of the deformed wrist, inevitably doubts crept in. A visit to the orthopaedic surgeon was all the reassurance I needed. Although my wrist was six months from being fully healed, it was not going to improve significantly over the coming weeks. It was a calculated gamble to play, but one I was willing to take.

The day before the Luton game, I was taken aside by the manager and the coach, Mick Hennigan, after training. I would have to prove my fitness by performing a few diving headers. Up until this point I had not fallen on my damaged arm and was not relishing the prospect. I was about to find out whether the injury had left any mental scars, something the manager was keen to find out as well. Five or six diving headers later, I was stopped by the manager and asked if I wanted to play the following day. I did not need to be asked twice. I walked out of the ground confidently looking forward to my return. It seemed a long time since my last outing and I was more than ready to get involved once again. It was then that a seed of doubt was sown in my mind. One of the club doctors, obviously concerned for my welfare, expressed doubts over my early return. It had after all been only six and a half weeks after suffering a double fracture. His intervention was well meant, but was the last thing I needed.

We reported prior to the game at 10.30 a.m., a little earlier than usual. This was to enable us to rehearse set-piece plays after being informed of the team selection. It was revealed that Eric Cantona, who had played in the previous draw at Everton, was omitted from the team. He was obviously extremely disappointed at the news, and barely spoke a word thereafter, not that anyone would have understood him. He spoke the bare minimum of English, and while I speak some French, it's nothing to get excited about. At times he looked almost suicidal as he moped around the dressing room area. From my time in France, I knew just how isolated he felt. Being dropped is bad enough, but when it is in a strange country, and you don't speak the language, it is considerably worse.

By this time I was feeling more than a little apprehensive. Although I was going to play with the protection of a plastic cast on my arm, I was not sure if I my decision to play had been the right one. One thing was certain, once I had crossed the white line, there could be no excuses, and that is the same for any professional, injury or no injury.

Luton, fighting for their First Division lives, had worked very hard to prevent us from scoring. Then, in the second half, Eric was brought on. It broke the pattern of the game up, and allowed us to score twice in the final twenty minutes. Eric's face was a picture of joy as he turned away from scoring his first goal for the club. What a contrast it made to his mood shortly before the kick off. I ran to him and was greeted with a joyous interpretation of my name: 'Shappee!' It brought a big smile to my face. Shortly afterwards I was experiencing the same level of elation as Eric had, when I volleyed home from twelve yards – my comeback had been justified.

Yet again the top position had changed hands as the end of February saw Manchester United having played the same number of matches as us, but two points better off. We knew that from now to the end of the season, every success or failure would be blown up out of all proportion by a media looking for crucial turning points in the championship race. The first was at home to Aston Villa when we stumbled to a goal-less draw. Gordon Strachan had missed a late penalty and was already being described by the press as the villain who might have cost Leeds the title. We all knew this to be ludicrous. Gordon's miss would prove no more decisive than a missed chance thirty games ago, when we were commencing the marathon of the English season.

We were aware that Manchester United were now very much in the stronger position. We also knew that we could not give up hope, we could still pull it round. There were some encouraging signs emerging from across the Pennines. In the goal-scoring department, United quite clearly had a dependency on Brian McClair. Mark Hughes's lack of goals was becoming increasingly apparent. Most important of all, every time we had given United a chance to pull away, they had failed to grab their opportunity.

Our next match at Spurs brought me back to the scene of my terrible facial injury. I gave it only a passing thought, for I had something more important on my mind – the championship. After our failure in midweek, it was vital for us to secure a win. This we did, 3–1, although it was a far from convincing performance. Winning when not playing well is thought to be a hallmark of champions. In the English First Division this certainly has some validity. The sheer quantity of matches means it is not physically possible to play well in all of them. A championship-winning team will inevitably, at times, have to rely on the confidence and positive attitude that comes from winning matches to see them through.

One setback from our victory was the injury to Mel Sterland. He had been carrying an ankle injury for some time and had only continued playing with the aid of painkilling injections. Now it had been damaged so severely it would require immediate surgery, something that would rule him out for the rest of the season. Much had been made of Manchester United's bad luck with injuries; it seemed that we were having worse luck. Gordon Strachan's recurring problem with sciatica only added to the manager's selection problems. Gary Speed and Gary McAllister were both tried at right back, a move that disturbed the balance of the team.

This disruption definitely played a major part in the ensuing run of only one win in five matches. In the first of these games at QPR, we were soundly thrashed 4–1. To make things worse, Chris Whyte was given his marching orders for what was deemed a 'professional' foul. The game mirrored the previous year's encounter when Gordon Strachan had been sent off during a crushing defeat. QPR were at the time the form team in the division and had already beaten Manchester United 4–1 at Old Trafford, only two months earlier.

Again we showed our resilience to bounce back in the following game against Wimbledon. I scored three of the goals in our 5–1 win, thus becoming only the sixth Leeds player – and only the second post-war – to score a trio of First Division hat tricks. It also confirmed that my rehabilitation was complete.

We moved on to Highbury to play Arsenal in front of the television cameras in a game from which we were disappointed to come away with only a point. Our encounters with Arsenal are always highly competitive tactical games with no quarter given, and this one was no different. When I snatched a goal against my old club with just over ten minutes to play, we felt sure it would be the winner. It was not to be, and the Gunners grabbed a late equaliser when a certain centre forward played their strikers onside.

The next match, at home to West Ham, was a source of further disappointment for the team and especially for myself. As was often the case, the visiting team to Elland Road were turned on by the occasion and raised their game accordingly. Their Czech goalkeeper, Ludek Miklosko, made many fine saves after suffering a string of blunders in his recent games.

Early in the first half, all his good work should have been rendered irrelevant. David Batty broke clear on the right and pulled a ball back along the six-yard box. I had broken free from my marker and had the ball in my sights. After scoring four goals in the two previous matches I was confident and relaxed – too much so as it turned out. I made contact with the ball, expecting to look up and find it nestling in the back of the net. To my horror, I saw the ball sail agonisingly wide of the post. Ninety-nine times out of a hundred a chance like that would have been dealt with effortlessly. The one time it was not could not have come at a worse time in the championship race. I was filled with annoyance at myself. It was the sort of thing that, earlier in my career, I might have allowed to affect my performance. All good strikers miss sitters. The reason they are good is that they do not miss them often, and when they do they carry on regardless – there will always be another chance. Unfortunately for me, there was not one in this game, which finished 0–0. That evening I relived the chance many times over, the ball finishing in the goal each time. Now it was my turn to be labelled the villain. There were six matches to go but it did not stop the media from labelling this missed chance the one that would cost Leeds the championship. I knew that was ludicrous, but I was also aware that if we lost the title by one or two points, much would be made of it.

We reported for training on the Monday, only to be told we were going to Harrogate Turkish Baths for a relaxing morning of sauna and massage. The following day Manchester United easily overcame a weakened Norwich side to finish March at the head of the table by a point, with a game in hand. Saturday's game against Manchester City suddenly gained extra significance.

It turned out to be one of those days when nothing goes right. City were deserving winners, but not by a margin of four goals. Without our missed chances and good saves by Tony Coton, a fairer result would have been 4–3. The mood in the dressing room afterwards was as sombre as it had ever been. United were now a point ahead, but more importantly they had two games in hand. They now had a chance to go seven points clear. The question was – could they take it?

Their first opportunity came three days later against Manchester City at Old Trafford. Things looked bad for us when City went one down and had Neil Pointon sent off. Unbelievably, City came back to draw 1–1, and even had a late chance to win. This was the first significant result in the final phase and gave our players a great boost. A United victory would have dealt Leeds a major blow. Now not only did United fail to win, they had lost a lead at home to ten men and were showing signs of not being able to handle the intense pressure both teams were under. Alex Ferguson in his after-match comments described the result as 'a killer – we had the chance to put some daylight between us and Leeds and we did not do it'. Little did he know then how much of a killer.

Prior to this result our mood was far from buoyant. We knew that United were the clear favourites and we needed them to falter. We had reported for training on the Monday and undergone a gruelling training session – no Turkish baths this time! The following day, I had arranged to go for lunch with Eric Cantona and Gary McAllister. Eric was on his own and it was time he sampled some of the culinary delights of North Yorkshire. The word got out, and the quiet lunch for three became a noisy one for twelve at the excellent Tannin Level in Harrogate. It was just what we all needed after the depressing events of the weekend. As the burgundy and banter flowed, fuelled by my wine-buff friend Peter Hopkins, it seemed we did not have that many problems after all. The lunch had drifted into the afternoon and had been very therapeutic for all concerned. As the result of the Manchester derby filtered through, it became almost a perfect day.

It was around this time that the respective managers, Howard Wilkinson and Alex Ferguson, were coming under very close scrutiny. They were obviously feeling intense pressure as the championship race drew to a close. Both men were within a few games of winning the greatest prize in English football, one which neither club had won for many years – eighteen in Leeds' case and twenty-five in United's. Both clubs had been yearning for a return to the halcyon years of the Revie and Busby eras. The ghosts of players like Bremner, Giles and Lorimer for Leeds, or Charlton and Law for United would soon have to be laid to rest.

Our routine at this stage was very much the same as it had been all season. Wilf Paish, the athletics coach, was brought in to vary the training once a week. Wilf had been working with the Olympic middle-distance runner, Peter Elliott, among others, and his training was a diversion from our normal sessions.

For his part, the manager was exuding relaxed confidence. He was going about his business as he always did and, to all intents and purposes, we could have been in a mid-table position. He stressed to us continually that all we could do was to give our best, and things would take care of themselves. Even after our heavy defeats at QPR and Manchester City, the subsequent pep talks were in no way overanimated. On both occasions he stressed our achievement in getting to the position we were in, adding that it was inevitable we would suffer setbacks, but that we must not let them affect our future performances.

The behaviour of Alex Ferguson seemed very different. He was showing distinct signs of inner turmoil. His team had always been favourites for the title and the subsequent pressure this brought from the media, and more importantly the supporters, appeared to have a detrimental effect. We were hearing rumours that United were already compiling their championship video and making plans for the cameras to enter the dressing room immediately after they had clinched the title.

Meanwhile, mischievous reports were appearing in the press about our players: Gary McAllister was supposedly moving to Rangers for £3 million and Howard Wilkinson was reputedly unhappy with centre halves Chris Fairclough and Chris Whyte. We were reliably informed, or so we thought, that these unsettling rumours had originated from across the Pennines.

Such speculation, however, only served to increase our resolve and we approached our following game, at home to Chelsea, with even more determination. United were now two points ahead, with a game in hand. Victory over Chelsea would take us back to the top, with United playing in the Rumbelows Cup Final the following day.

In the event we were comfortable 3–0 winners, with the high-light of the game coming in the form of a wonderful goal from Eric Cantona. Receiving the ball on the corner of the Chelsea penalty area, he took it in his stride, flicked it up twice, taking it past two defenders, and then unleashed a glorious right-foot volley into the top left-hand corner of the goal. It was comparable with the finest goals of George Best, Duncan McKenzie or Frank Worthington, the last two of whom briefly played for Leeds. Eric had formed a great rapport with the fans, and their chants of 'Oooh – Aah – Can – tona!' were to become a regular feature of our games. He was proving to be more effective when brought on as a late substitute. The French football he had been used to allows players time to dwell on the ball. In England space usually only begins to appear later in the second half. Eric had not yet adapted to the hectic pace of first-half English football, but his lik-ing for receiving the ball in space and running at defences was proving highly effective each time he was brought on.

We were now a point ahead of United, having played two games more. A betting man would have put his money on our rivals, but we were gradually becoming more and more confident. We knew United had an almost impossible schedule of four games in seven days over the Easter period and that this would prove decisive.

Their first game resulted in a win against Southampton. Although it took them back to the top of the table, their lack of goals was an encouraging sign. To add to this, injuries to Bryan Robson and Paul Ince meant that they would struggle to be fit for the remaining fixtures.

Two days later at Luton they squandered a 1–0 half-time lead to draw 1–1. Meanwhile we were at Liverpool, a game everyone was saying we had to win. The home team had raised their game and were playing as well as they had done all season. We had gone to Anfield for a win, but were happy to come away with a goal-less draw. The result seemed even better when we returned to the dressing room to hear that Luton had equalised. As we left the pitch the Liverpool players were wishing us well and hoping that we would win the title. This feeling was echoed by home support-ers as we left the ground. 'Don't let that lot down the road win it!' was a common sentiment. It all augured well for the following Sunday when Liverpool would play our rivals.

On Easter Monday afternoon, United were at home to Nott-ingham Forest. It was Forest's fifty-ninth game of the season, and they had recently completed a gruelling schedule in an attempt to clear their backlog of fixtures. It put United's tiredness into perspective.

We were playing at home to Coventry in a live televised match at 5 p.m. As we entered the dressing room an hour before the kick off, we were told that Forest had taken an early lead, although United soon equalised. We ran out for the warm-up trying to concentrate on what we had to do. It was twenty minutes before the start and the ground was almost full. Suddenly an almighty roar erupted from the Kop. It could mean only one thing – Forest had gone ahead. A buzz immediately ran through the players – it was a tremendous feeling.

When we returned to the dressing room it was confirmed. My old club Forest had beaten United 2–1. The winning goal had been scored by Scot Gemmill, who had been an apprentice during my time at the club. Some had doubted whether he would make it at the top level. Now, not only was he blossoming into a fine young player, but he was going to be fondly remembered by Leeds fans for a long time to come. We ran back on to the pitch in a highly charged state. Coventry put up brave resistance, but were eventually overpowered 2–0. We were back on top of the League by a point. We had enjoyed the advantage of knowing the United result prior to the kick off this time. A week later, the roles would be reversed.

Despite our lead, however, Manchester United were still slight favourites, as they travelled to West Ham to complete their seven-day programme. West Ham were almost relegated and had also been involved in a backlog of fixtures. In fact United's four opponents during the Easter period had all been embroiled in similar fixture congestion. Victory would have put United clear by two points with two games to play; a draw or defeat for them would leave us in pole position. As the evening approached, it almost felt as if I was playing the match. In a futile attempt to distract our attention from the game at Upton Park, we had arranged for club solicitor Peter McCormick and his wife Kathryn to come round for dinner.

Shortly before we sat down to eat, I paged Teletext for the latest score. Unbelievably United were trailing 1–0 to a Kenny Brown goal, but with over half an hour still to play. Could Kenny Brown join Scot Gemmill as an unwitting Leeds folk hero? The tension was unbearable. The conversation did not hold our full attention as we anxiously waited for the final whistle. I could not wait any longer and was about to page Teletext once again when the telephone rang. It was my mother-in-law, Elly, calling to tell me United had lost. A roar erupted from the dinner table and an extra bottle was opened in celebration.

For the first time in the season, our destiny was in our own hands. If we could win our two remaining matches we would be crowned the League champions.

As everybody had focused their attention on the dogfight between ourselves and United, Sheffield Wednesday had crept up unnoticed and were now in a position to snatch the title away from us. A win for them at Crystal Palace on the Saturday in their penultimate match of the season would see them overtake United and draw level on points with Leeds, as both our games were to be played on the Sunday. It seemed there would be an extra twist in the tale, with Wednesday a goal up with only two minutes remaining. Then a typical Palace punt upfield found Mark Bright, who equalised and in so doing dashed any hopes Wednesday may have had. At least they had the consolation of qualification for the UEFA Cup.

As Wednesday made their long trek home, we were heading for the same destination, to play one of the most important matches in the club's history. Victory against the other Sheffield club, United, the following day could establish us as champions, provided Manchester United lost at Liverpool three hours later.

We had spent the morning rehearsing set-piece plays and as usual before matches against Sheffield United it was an extensive session. The two managers, Howard Wilkinson and Dave Bassett, are particularly good friends. It is a relationship that creates a keen rivalry as both managers try to put one over on each other. This, combined with the importance of the match, only served to intensify our preparation.

Our normal routine was adhered to as we booked into the hotel and gathered for dinner. The signs were good. Nobody seemed uptight and the conversation was very relaxed. The normal meal of various pastas was eagerly consumed before everybody retired to bed. I slept well that night and dreamt pleasantly of the following day and what might be.

The twelve o'clock kick off meant we barely had time to take breakfast and assemble for our pre-match meeting. The manager's team talk was calm, collected and very matter of fact. This was not the time for a Churchillian day-of-destiny speech. We all knew the importance of the game, and any further motivation could have proved inhibitive.

We reached the ground only to find an army of journalists and television crews between us and the away dressing room. Once inside, we began to prepare for battle, one hour later. Each player has his own individual routine which he uses for every match. All players initially change and then go through their favourite stretching exercises. Some players have an active preparation, while others sit quietly reading the match programme. The younger players like David Batty and Gary Speed tend to be more animated, whereas those at the opposite end of the age scale, like John Lukic, Gordon Strachan and myself, tend to have a more relaxed routine. After a few years in the game, most professionals instinctively know their best preparation for a match.

The atmosphere among the players was very encouraging. Jokes were being cracked and legs pulled, just like they had been for the previous forty games. Reserve player Dylan Kerr took the brunt of our humour. Dylan is notorious for his ability to appear in photographs, especially those of a celebratory nature. It seemed he was preparing to do so again.

The game began in a highly charged atmosphere, with both sets of fans responding to the occasion. Sheffield were on a roll, the form team of the division, and were doing us no favours. They went ahead through Alan Cork and as half-time approached, things were not going well for us. The home crowd even taunted us with 'You're gonna win fuck all!' With only a few minutes of the first half remaining, I was fouled as I rose for a header. Gordon Strachan, as alert as ever, quickly took the kick, to the surprise of the Sheffield defence. He fed the ball to Rod Wallace who was in the clear. The keeper raced out to block and was injured in the process and the ball squirted to Gary Speed, whose shot was deflected off Brian Gayle, on to Rod Wallace and into the net. It was the first of three bizarre goals that afternoon and one that came at a vital moment. We returned to the dressing room with a much-needed boost.

Early in the second half Jon Newsome, back in his home city, scored from a set-piece play, when the injured keeper came for a cross, only to miss it, allowing Jon to head into an empty goal. The Leeds fans were sent into raptures by a player few had even heard of a year earlier. To our dismay, this goal was soon followed by a Sheffield equaliser. Their corners had been a constant problem throughout the match and as another swung over, John Pemberton was left unmarked beyond the far post. The ball seemed to be going out when he hooked it quickly back towards the goal and directly at me. Once again I displayed some of my clinical finishing inside the six-yard box by turning the ball into my own goal. I was horrified and with this added to my early booking for dangerous play, it did not look like being my day.

We had been through many setbacks during our long and arduous campaign. This was just another and I knew we were capable of overcoming it. What I did not foresee was the bizarre way in which we would do it. Brian Gayle, chasing on to a lofted pass, proceeded to bounce the ball off his thigh and head it over his own keeper and into the unguarded goal. As the final whistle blew, players and supporters alike jumped for joy. It was the first time we had won twice in a row since Christmas, and it could not have come at a more critical time.

Back in the dressing room we felt a mixture of joy and disbelief at the strange events of the afternoon. Fortune had favoured us just when we needed it most. As I left the haven of the dressing room I was immediately set upon by TV and press. I could not claim the title: I had been in the game long enough to realise that anything was still possible. It was also not a time to gloat. We had performed in a very professional manner without ever excelling ourselves, and had come away with an all-important victory.

The coach journey home was a very strange affair. We were in limbo, not knowing the full significance of our result. We had done all we could: now we would have to sit back and see if Liverpool could do the rest for us. ITV had wanted to install cameras inside my house and film the reactions of myself and other players to the result at Anfield. I had agreed to let them in only if we were victorious at Bramall Lane and in no other circumstances. As we travelled up the M1 I received a call on my mobile phone from ITV's Trevor East who was in charge of *The Match*. United had gone a goal down early in the first half – so far so good.

The coach journey over, I raced home, eager to view the remainder of the game. Until then the car radio would have to do, however frustrating it was. When I arrived back my house looked more like a film set than a home. Technicians and equipment were everywhere.

As I sat there with Eric Cantona, David Batty and Gary

McAllister watching the last throes of the Manchester United challenge, it did not seem proper to whoop it up as ITV wanted us to do. We had been dignified and professional all season, and it would have been uncharacteristic for us to be any different now. We knew the roles could have been reversed and it would have been wrong to gloat over United's demise. When the final whistle sounded and we realised we had won the greatest honour in the English game, it was something of an anticlimax. We had not won it directly as a result of our victory earlier that day – that would have been different. Our adrenalin levels had now subsided and it was difficult to get overexcited. That would come later. We were also slightly shocked and a little numb. As the day began, we knew the outcome was possible, but no one dared believe it could happen. It had seemed inevitable that the championship would go to the very last game.

As the cameras were being switched off the phone started ringing and was not to stop for two days. Friends and relatives called non-stop to congratulate me, and the team, on our achievement. Out of nowhere, a crowd of well-wishers descended upon my house with gifts of champagne. Later that evening all the local players met in an Italian restaurant in Leeds, The Flying Pizza, to celebrate our success. As we entered, the whole of the restaurant rose and gave us a five-minute standing ovation. It was a wonderful reception and one that made us realise just how much our success meant to everybody in Leeds. The party, which continued long into the night, was an experience none of us will forget. Outside the whole city was buzzing with excitement. Car horns were blaring and people were singing and dancing in the streets in scenes of wild revelry.

My only regret was that my late father, Roy, could not be present to witness it all. He had died when my career was at a desperately low point during my days at Arsenal – a time when it seemed nigh on impossible that I would ever experience a day such as this.

There were some who questioned whether we had been deserving of our success. It was said that rather than Leeds winning the title, Manchester United had lost it. It is true that United's backlog of fixtures had been significant, especially the period of four matches in seven days, although it must be reiterated that their opponents during those seven days had all undergone a similarly gruelling programme. We had finished the season with a goal tally bettered only by Arsenal, as well as suffering only one defeat in the first half of the season, and just four overall, the same number as the Leeds team of Bremner, Giles, Clarke et al., in their championship campaign of 1973–74. Both teams had to grapple with the burden of a glorious past, and this was the deciding factor in the championship race. We had coped with ours, but United had found theirs much more frightening than they had ever imagined.

With all the pressure off, the final match at home to Norwich was one to savour and enjoy. There was a wonderful party atmosphere as the League trophy was presented to our captain, Gordon Strachan, to hold aloft. As it was passed to me and I raised it into the air, I noticed I was carrying it with my bandaged left arm. My injury had now healed sufficiently for me to bear the trophy's weight. That grim night in January seemed a long time ago.

· 2 ·

Football in the blood

It was almost inevitable that I would eventually become a professional footballer. Even my birthplace was a sign of things to come – Scorer Street, a kick away from Lincoln City Football Club – and the whole of my childhood was spent in a football environment. My father, Roy, had a distinguished career as an inside forward in the lower divisions of the Football League, scoring over two hundred goals, before moving into management, and my mother, Gill, was secretary to five managers at Stoke City during the 1970s and early 1980s.

My father began his career with Aston Villa during their successful years in the fifties. He signed for them in 1953, as an eighteen-year-old from Kynoch's Works team, where he was working in the munitions factory. During his five-year stay he made nineteen appearances in the First Division and scored eight goals, including one on his first-team debut against Middlesbrough. Also on Villa's books at that time was a promising youngster called Ron Atkinson, who had signed from BSA Tools of the Birmingham Works League shortly after my father. The two were to remain friends for many years, both as players and as managers.

Players in those days were certainly not in the game for the money. Although wanting for nothing, my childhood days were not filled with opulence. The family's early accommodation was terraced, and even on his retirement, my father could afford only a modest semi-detached house. If money was not his motivation, then his love for the game certainly was. His dedication and professionalism are things which remain with me to this day. One of my earliest childhood memories is from the mid-sixties when, aged five, I was making an excessive amount of noise along with my three-year-old sister, Denise. Unbeknown to us, this was the afternoon before an evening home match, and my father was taking his pre-match nap, a ritual which remains with players to this day. Not surprisingly, our racket woke my father, and he was not amused. We were shortly experiencing his wrath, a thing that was to persuade us in the future to remain silent on such occasions.

It was around this time that my father began taking me with him to work. He was in his second spell at Lincoln City, and had been recently appointed player-manager after four years at Mansfield. I had the run of the ground, but the highlight of every visit was being allowed to play on the fruit machine in the social club. I remember it being like a scene from Michael Palin's *Golden Gordon*, a TV comedy about a terminally bad football team; a few diehards would turn up for a pint and occasionally give me sixpence for another game. The football environment seemed commonplace to me – I could take it or leave it. The real excitement was to come later.

My father's short-lived career as player-manager meant that we were on the move again. He was transferred to Port Vale and we were transferred to a club house in Trentham, Stoke-on-Trent. This at least meant stability. Although my father was to work for several more clubs as a player and a manager, I was to remain in this house until I left home at the age of nineteen.

I started attending my new junior school and my football education began. The sports master, Mr Dale, was a very keen football man, and his enthusiasm spread throughout the school. He was a stern disciplinarian with dark Brylcreemed hair. He was of the old-school type and looked decidedly out of place in his tracksuit and football boots. His views on the game were uncompromising and his young disciples, naturally, obeyed his every command. Members of his junior and senior teams were looked upon as heroes and treated accordingly. This game of football had something going for it after all.

I was soon chosen for the junior team and enjoying all its fringe benefits. One such benefit was my first bonus scheme in football. Every member of the junior or senior team, if on the winning side, was allowed a sixpence or shilling's worth of sweets, depending on the importance of the victory. Mr Dale would send carefully selected girls to classrooms during lessons on Monday morning, and orders would be given in front of the class with great relish.

I was soon to learn that life in football was not all sweets. During an end-of-season cup final, I was given the job of taking a match-winning penalty. Glory was to be mine with only minutes to play. The unthinkable happened – I missed! We went on to lose in extra time. I was still crying an hour later. Many years on I was to learn that football had even greater highs than bags of sweets and much deeper lows than missed penalties.

It was about this time that I was starting to enjoy the spectacle of football, if only in a small way. My mother would take me to watch my father playing for Port Vale in home matches. Port Vale were managed by the legendary Sir Stanley Matthews. Unfortunately Sir Stan was not having the success he enjoyed as a player, and his team were languishing in the lower half of the Fourth Division, attracting crowds of only three or four thousand. This meagre turnout was made to look even worse by the sheer size of Vale Park. Vast empty spaces were not only very evident, but contributed greatly to a lack of atmosphere.

I remember vividly the smell of liniment and rubbing oil around the tunnel area and these hugely powerful men emerging to take part in a game far removed from the one I played. I was quickly bored during matches and counted away the minutes until I could raid the sandwiches in the family room at half-time and full-time. This boredom arose not only from the subdued atmosphere, but also from my lack of years. Fourth Division football was a little hard for a ten-year-old to appreciate.

I would occasionally be taken by my father to training, where I was allowed to have a bath with the players. It was a huge communal bath, one I could barely stand up in. I was in awe of these men as I nervously washed. Their physical presence was quite frightening, and I was always relieved to emerge from the water in one piece.

I was starting to become aware of footballing events. I watched on television as Manchester United beat Benfica 4–1 in the European Cup final. I now had a team to support and heroes to go with it. Bobby Charlton and George Best were to remain my idols for some time. I soon posted my autograph book to Old Trafford for the team's signatures, only to be severely disappointed when it was returned with printed autographs. Even someone of my tender years could tell the players had not really signed it themselves.

After two years at Port Vale, my father was transferred to Chester. We didn't move house and my father made the eighty mile round trip each day. Initially, he would take me to home matches, but things did not work out. He was thirty-four years old and

approaching the end of his career. As with any seasoned professional, it must have been a depressing and worrying time. My
father had only known the world of football, and might have
imagined his playing days would last forever. Now they were end-
ing, he must have considered his future with great trepidation.

I stopped going to matches, he was dropped and after one season he was transferred again. This time it was to non-league
Nuneaton Borough. It was the end of his playing career in the
Football League and not far from the end of his playing career at
any level. Looking back, I can now understand why I was not
taken to further matches. My father was a proud man and the
realisation that he could no longer play League football must
indeed have been a sad one. Although every professional knows
that one day he will play his final match at that level, this knowledge does not prepare him for its eventuality. For many players it
is something to be pushed to the back of their minds in the hope
that it may never happen.

I am sure my father must have seen the end coming, but football
was his life. He had spent almost twenty years in the game as a
player and was ill-equipped for life outside it. For most players the
options were to run a pub, open a sports shop, or stay in the
game. My father chose to stay, and after a few months at
Nuneaton Borough moved into management with Stafford
Rangers in the Northern Premier League.

Around the same time, I began supporting my local team. Stoke
City were a better-than-average First Division side with a reputation for playing attractive football. I first followed them during the
1970-71 season when their great FA Cup run ended sadly against
Arsenal in the semi-finals. Two games were needed to separate the
teams. The first was held at Hillsborough, a game I watched from
the Leppings Lane End. It seemed certain that Stoke were on their
way to Wembley as they led 2–1 in injury time. A dramatic finale
saw John Mahoney handle the ball on the Stoke goal-line, directly
in front of us. Peter Storey duly converted the penalty and the tie
went to a replay, a game Stoke were to lose. It was a tragic day for
a twelve-year-old, but real tragedy was to strike in this very spot
many years later.

The following year, I was more fortunate, visiting Wembley
twice in one season. The first time was the occasion of the FA
Non-League Challenge Trophy Final. My father had started to
work wonders by turning Stafford Rangers into a non-League

force. The 1972 final saw them playing Barnet in front of 34,000 people.

I travelled to London on the Friday with my brother, sister and mother. The following day we saw Stafford triumph 3–0 in a very exciting final. The after-match scenes were indeed jubilant, climaxing in a reception at the Hotel Russell. I remember my brother and sister and I sneaking out way after our bedtime to try and witness the frantic celebrations. Our attempts were futile and we were led back to our room by an indignant porter after locking ourselves out. The following day we travelled back with the team and were paraded around Stafford in an open-top bus, cheered by huge crowds. It was an exhilarating experience. Although my father was to repeat this feat seven years later, this must have been his proudest football moment.

My second visit to Wembley was only weeks later. My 'real' team, Stoke City, were to beat Chelsea 2–1 in the final of the League Cup. This time the stadium was full to its 100,000 capacity and the atmosphere was completely different. I had forgotten about Best and Charlton; my new heroes were the likes of Gordon Banks, Peter Dobing, George Eastham and John Ritchie. A bond was forged, and my links with the club, firstly as a supporter, then as a player, were to last for a further eleven years.

My mother became secretary to Stoke manager Tony Waddington at about the same time. This enabled me to receive complimentary tickets to all home matches. My attendance at the Victoria Ground was to become a ritual for many years to come.

The match atmosphere was one I revelled in. I can still recall how my excitement began as I travelled by car to the ground. The walk from our parking place to the periphery of the ground increased the excitement further. A quick stop at the sweet shop for a quarter of our favourite boiled sweets, then the swell of the crowd around the turnstiles edged my expectancy level up a little more until I finally entered that hallowed arena. The powerful smell of warm pies and Bovril instantly hit me as I bought my programme and located my seat, all the while absorbing the atmosphere inside the ground.

The pre-match talk was always about who should play and who should not . . . How they could have played so badly in their previous game . . . The size of the away team's following . . . How we were certainly going to win today. . . . Then the teams emerged to a roar of sound. The team was analysed during the kick in and selection discussed. The game kicked off and every ball was then played mentally, as if I was on the field. It was indeed a draining experience. A home goal was greeted with elation, an away goal with dejection. Win or lose, the game was always dissected on my journey home with my friend and father. Disagreements were inevitable, but we always agreed to be there for the next one.

My visits to the Victoria Ground enabled me to form my first impressions of Leeds United. They were experiencing their glory days of the seventies, under Don Revie, and were the team everybody wanted to beat. This was largely because they were probably the best team at the time, but it was also partly due to the fact that they were not a well-liked side. Leeds had a reputation for arrogance, ruthlessness and downright dirty play. If you were not a Leeds supporter it was fashionable at the time to dislike them intensely. I was not a Leeds supporter.

During the 1973-74 season, Leeds had remained unbeaten for their first twenty-nine matches. They arrived at the Victoria Ground seemingly invincible, ready to take yet another scalp on their march to the title. The ground was full, the cameras were there and the level of expectancy was enormous. Stoke, as they were capable of doing, raised their game to rarely seen heights and completely outplayed their formidable opposition. After trailing 2–0, Stoke staged an incredible comeback with goals from Mike Pejic, Alan Hudson and Denis Smith, to finish 3–2 winners. Leeds were obviously affected by this result and lost three of their last twelve matches. They narrowly won the title, but with a comparatively low total of sixty-two points.

I was very much aware of Leeds' success during the seventies – how could you fail to be? For all their undoubted qualities, it was strange how they fell at the final hurdle so many times, failing to win the trophies many felt they should have done. It was also apparent how few friends they gained along the way. Talk to any old professional who played against them and he will talk of the 'nasty' players the Leeds team contained. The midfield area in particular provided the hard element; Billy Bremner and Johnny Giles were renowned as players not to be trifled with. The universal dislike of the team made them even stronger as a unit.

A natural reaction by many minority groups in the face of ill feeling and prejudice is to close ranks and become insular. Leeds at the time were a minority group and behaved in the same manner. This strength was emphasised in their reputed policy of looking after each other on the field. If, for instance, Allan Clarke had been badly fouled and injured, the offending person would have been noted by the Leeds players. Shortly afterwards the offender would, so I was told, be on the receiving end of the same treatment, by a player other than Clarke.

This dislike of Leeds, I am sure, was also the reason for their failures. Teams playing at Leeds would raise their game just that bit more, especially in the crucial matches. Players, after all, are only human, and dislike is a great motivating factor. It was very much a case of 'We don't care who wins it, as long as it isn't Leeds.'

It's nice to know that this time round, Leeds' success has been greeted in a much more positive manner. The current Leeds team have won many friends with their attractive, attacking football. The whole image of the club has changed. The hooligan element which was a throwback to the seventies has been controlled to such an extent that families are now visiting Elland Road once again. During the seventies it was fashionable for certain elements to become football hooligans. This, coupled with people's general dislike of Leeds, created a particularly bad problem at Elland Road. Leeds supporters carried this hooligan tag during the whole of the 1980s, up until very recently, but it has now been removed after painstaking efforts by everybody connected with the club.

A family stand was created to provide an area safe for both parents and children. This was followed by a campaign against racist chanting and bad language. Most important of all, it was the fans who stood up and let themselves be counted. Any initiative, although started by club officials, must be taken up by the supporters of the club. It is with great pride that the club can say it is now unfashionable to be a troublemaker at Elland Road.

Back in the early seventies, I never for one moment thought I would one day play for this great club. The football I was playing was light years away from the football I watched most Saturdays. I could dream, and dream I did. I was now in my teens at high school and making good progress, gaining selection for my town and county teams. It was while playing for these teams and my school that I acquired a burning desire – to become an 'associate schoolboy'. Boys just a little older than me were being signed on by professional clubs as associate schoolboys, and I saw no reason why I should not join their ranks. The two main local teams were Stoke City and Port Vale. It was no contest; Stoke it had to be. But however much I wanted it to happen, it was not going to happen immediately.

Not having a connection with a League club enabled me to train with my father's team, Stafford Rangers. They were a part-time club who trained on Tuesday and Thursday evenings. At the time, Stafford were arguably the best non-League team in the country, containing a mixture of ex-League players who were on their way down, and players who were just not quite good enough for the top level. I really was stepping up from school football. At first I was out of my depth and quite bewildered by it all. This did not last for long and my twice-weekly visits saw big improvements in my game. I soon began enjoying myself, so much so, in fact, that these two evenings became the highlights of my week.

The atmosphere and spirit among these part-time players was probably the best I have known. Everybody would meet in the social club after training sessions and often progress from there to town for a night out. Competition for places was keen but very civilised, with no ill feeling between players. This is rarely the case at professional clubs; the difference here was the financial factor. All the players had full-time jobs – decorators, window-cleaners, mechanics, even civil servants – and played football not for the small wage they received, but for the sheer joy of playing. It is inevitable that at the professional level, when livelihoods are at stake, competition becomes much fiercer.

On a purely financial basis, many teams in what is now the Third Division I believe would be better off operating on a part-time basis. Barnet have led the way in showing that part-timers can compete at the highest levels of the division. I am convinced we have too many full-time professional clubs operating in this country. If football is to have a healthy future, I think it is essential that clubs are run on a viable financial basis. Too many clubs, for too long, have existed on the verge of bankruptcy. Several clubs recently have been existing on a week-to-week basis, with no one knowing if they have a future or not. How can that be beneficial for the future of our game?

The last thing I want to see is fellow professionals losing their jobs, but in many cases players would be financially better off – both now and in the future, after their football careers have finished – if they took a full-time job. Many of the lower-division players are on very paltry wages, with no immediate job alternative if their football careers were to finish suddenly. Part-time football is, I believe, the answer to these problems, not for every club but certainly for many. A move to part-time football would guarantee the future of many struggling clubs. This, coupled with a regionalisation of the lower divisions, would help further still. A northern and southern regionalisation would guarantee a marked reduction in operating costs and an increased revenue due to a larger number of local derbies and the improved attendance figures these matches would produce.

My involvement with Stafford Rangers helped me enormously. I played for their reserve team on several occasions and gradually saw my game improving. Then one day, my mother returned from work bearing the news I had dreamed of hearing. The current manager, Tony Waddington, to whom she happened to be secretary, had asked her permission to sign me on associate schoolboy forms. After such a long wait, I received the news with a mixture of joy and disbelief. It was a great moment for me, although the hard work was only just beginning.

I started to attend midweek training sessions along with other non-contract players and trialists. The objective was to break into Stoke's fourth team, a daunting task considering the number attending those sessions. After a frustrating wait, I was eventually given my chance. I was fortunate to have the fourth-team coach firmly in my corner. George Jackson had tragically been forced to end a promising professional career in his mid-twenties while playing for Stoke City. He was now involved as a coach and gave me every encouragement in those difficult early days. Whatever age or level a player attains, it is always important to have such a figure behind him.

Although I was heavily involved with the game, my academic life did not take a back seat. It was not obvious, certainly to me, that my future lay in professional football. As my sixteenth birthday approached, I was studying for eight O levels. I was not the most dedicated of students, but I was always aware of the importance of good qualifications. Revision for exams was always left to the last possible moment and in this respect I was fortunate to have a photographic memory. I passed seven of my eight O levels and secured a place at the Stoke-on-Trent Sixth-Form College. I was to take A levels in mathematics, chemistry, biology and general studies. What I would do with these qualifications, I had no idea.

Although I did not realise it at the time, I had only one desire –

to become a professional footballer. Over sixteen years, football had seeped inexorably into my blood, if it had not been there to start with. The basic desire of a son to emulate his father had been the strongest motivation. My father's continued involvement, and that of my mother, at Stoke City, only enhanced this feeling. It really was a way of life to me, and to pursue another career would have gone against the grain.

I started my studies but continued my involvement with Stoke. The college had first call on my football services, but I still managed to turn out for Stoke's fourth team. I progressed to their third team and was even invited to train with the apprentices and young professionals whenever I could get time off from my studies. On one such occasion I turned up to train with the apprentices and noticed a full-scale practice game between the first team and the reserves taking place on the main pitch. I commenced training with the apprentices only to get a request for my services in the practice match. I had a sudden attack of nerves, the severity of which I had not experienced before. Little did I know this was the first of many such attacks over the following years. I was going into the unknown. I was actually going to play on the same pitch as First Division footballers, many of whom were my heroes. 'Up front for the reserves, son,' was the command. I nervously pulled on my bib and entered that hallowed arena. In a sense it did not seem real. I had sat in the stands and watched so many matches on this pitch, over so many years, it did not seem possible that I was now performing on it myself.

It was then that I surprised myself a little. Although barely controlling my nerves, my overriding instinct was to impress and seize my chance. I started to control my nervous energy and settled into the game. My first few lay-offs had gone well and within ten minutes I found myself bearing down on the first-team goal with only the goalkeeper to beat. This goalkeeper was a certain Peter Shilton. On this realisation I almost froze. He dived at my feet, I reacted and somehow managed to clip the ball over his body and into the far corner of the goal. I was ecstatic and shrieked in delight as I ran from the goal. What a moment! What a feeling!

This feeling was to become an addiction that I still have today. It is a feeling I shall never lose, nor want to. Whatever highs can be attained with artificial stimulants, surely they cannot compare with the highs I have experienced during my years of goalscoring. It will inevitably be something I shall sorely miss when the dreaded day comes when I can play no longer.

Shortly afterwards I was selected for the reserve team, and it was not long before I was playing with, and against, players I had admired from the stands. I had watched Terry Conroy, the Irish international, play in that epic FA Cup semi-final at Hillsborough many years earlier. He was now my striking partner and helping me in any way he could. It was a situation I sometimes found hard to believe.

My progress coincided with a major setback for my father. Five years of nonstop success as manager of Stafford Rangers had seen him become a desirable asset. He was offered the job of managing Stockport County – or so it seemed. The chairman of Stockport County was Freddie Pye, now involved with Manchester City. His idea of managing a club seemed to differ wildly from my father's. Like so many chairmen, especially at the lower levels, he seemed to think that the chairman should be actively involved in team selection, and the buying and selling of players. One such transaction acquired the services of George Best, in an attempt to boost attendance figures and improve a mediocre team. Crowds nearly doubled as people flocked to witness a genius among artisans. Sadly, George's great days were over and the experiment was short-lived.

My father's management reign was also short-lived, and he was sacked within a year. He was soon reappointed as manager of Stafford Rangers, however, and within a year the FA Challenge Trophy was won again, and the club gained entry to the newly formed Alliance Premier League. The following season saw a slump in fortunes, and despite the club's greatest period of success being achieved under my father, he was sacked in February 1980 for the final time.

I was no longer living at home and was very wrapped up in my own career. Even so my father's disappointment and damaged pride were plain to see. A brief period of coaching at Port Vale ensued. After failing to get further work in football he became a representative for a sports equipment firm and coached the company team in the Midlands League.

My college days ended with passes in all four A level subjects and I was offered a place at Manchester University to study for a degree in chemistry and business studies. I still had no idea where my future lay. Deep down, my only real desire was to become a professional footballer. My college studies were there as a safety net to protect me from failure in football. I had never seriously contemplated a career outside the game and my studies were taken without purpose.

My reserve outings for Stoke City had gone well, but not well enough to guarantee a contract, and after an anxious wait I was summoned to the office of the recently appointed manager, Alan Durban. I already knew that any visit to the manager's office was a matter for great trepidation. I nervously knocked at his door and was told to enter. I approached his desk like a nervous schoolboy approaching his headmaster. My fate was about to be revealed. The manager offered me a one-year contract at £40 per week. The thought of negotiating never entered my head and I eagerly accepted. I floated out of his office, hardly believing I was to become a real professional.

The contract was soon signed and my entry to university deferred for a year, just in case things did not work out. My future had suddenly become very clear indeed.

· 3 ·

Stoking the fire of ambition

When I signed professional forms, the last thing I expected was that my initial taste of first-team football would occur five months later, for a club over two hundred miles away. I had always imagined my debut would be with Stoke, the team I had supported for so many years. But shortly after my nineteenth birthday, Howard Kendall, who was player-coach with Stoke at the time, called me into the coaches' room and asked me if I would like to go on loan to Plymouth Argyle who were in the Third Division. When I was told that their manager was Malcolm Allison, and that he wanted to buy me, I eagerly accepted the opportunity.

Stoke were willing to let me go on loan and so enable me to obtain valuable League experience. In my eyes it was also a chance to work with probably the most talked-about manager of the day. The media image was of a flamboyant, champagne-drinking ladies' man who smoked Havana cigars and wore a fedora hat. He was also renowned for being an innovative, progressive coach, and his interest in me was extremely flattering.

I made the arduous train journey down to Plymouth, and on arrival was shown my accommodation for the next four weeks, a pleasant guest house a mile from Home Park. Already living there were two seasoned professionals, midfielder Barry Silkman, and goalkeeper Tony Burns, both worldly Londoners. Barry, especially, had been drawn to Plymouth purely by the attraction of Malcolm Allison. He was in fact to follow Malcolm after he was appointed manager of Manchester City, fifteen months later. Both players took me under their wing and made this strange new world very bearable. Tony was a great practical joker, with a wickedly dry sense of humour. Unfortunately his favourite trick was to lie in wait inside wardrobes or behind half-closed doors and leap out at unsuspecting victims uttering a piercing scream as he did so. The fact that more often that not he would be wearing a set of bloodied fangs made this a truly frightening experience. Within a few days I was deeply suspicious of places of concealment such as large items of furniture, and movement around the guest house became extremely nerve-racking.

Like many professionals in their thirties, Tony was a shrewd cynic – the antithesis of myself at that time. I was like any youngster coming into the game; naive, gullible and overenthusiastic, as Tony must have been when he first started out as a teenager with Arsenal. The transition from gullible to cynical seems to be a necessity to cope with the severe highs and lows every player experiences to a greater or lesser extent during his career. Although most types of jobs have this effect, in football the degree of change, I believe, is much greater.

My involvement with a first team was a great learning experience. Instead of mixing solely with players of my own age, I was working with experienced professionals of all ages. Two of the players in Plymouth's first team, goalkeeper Martin Hodge and midfielder Gary Megson, were to link up with me six years later at Sheffield Wednesday.

The first team coach at the time was Lennie Lawrence, later to become a successful manager at Charlton and Middlesbrough. Lennie was an obvious enthusiast who had to endure many snipes behind his back because of his lack of League experience. This is often the stock criticism made by players about coaches or managers who have not had a substantial League playing career. It is an extra burden for them to overcome and one Lennie has surmounted admirably.

My League debut came four days after my nineteenth birthday, on 9 December 1978, at home to Watford, who were then managed by the present England manager, Graham Taylor. They had won the Fourth Division title the previous season, and were on their meteoric rise from the Fourth to the First Division. They were one of the earliest sides in modern times to play the long-ball game, since adopted by many teams, such as Wimbledon, Crystal Palace and Sheffield United. The trailblazers were Graham Taylor's previous club, Lincoln, where it had also proved very successful.

Watford's side included ex-England coach Steve Harrison at left back, as well as Luther Blissett and Steve Sherwood. We were subjected to an aerial bombardment but managed to come out of the game with a creditable 1–1 draw. It was an exhilarating experience to play in front of a crowd of nearly twelve thousand instead of the hundreds I had been used to previously.

I will never forget how nervous I felt before that game. It seemed my anxiety would get the better of me, only for it to disappear minutes after the kick off. The game seemed to last a fraction of the ninety minutes I knew it must have gone on for. It was an important event, I performed satisfactorily, and that evening I wallowed in the thought that I could perform at League level, if only in the Third Division.

I was to play two further games before my return to Stoke, and my time at Plymouth enabled me to gain a valuable insight into the truth behind the image of Malcolm Allison. Far from being the extrovert character I had read about in the newspapers, I found him to be an introverted, almost shy person. His fedora hat was never seen, and only the occasional Havana cigar was ever smoked.

Malcolm's training sessions were always enjoyable and never repetitive. He was constantly innovative and always searching for something new. It was as a coach, I believe, that his great talent was best employed. As manager, with no one above him to say no, he would often be different just for the sake of being different. Football is a simple game, where winning teams are created by a combination of good players and strong leadership. Tactical changes are sometimes needed within a familiar team pattern. Malcolm would often change his team pattern entirely and complicate the game by constantly introducing systems that were alien to his players. It was a shame his later experience at Manchester City, where he had once been so successful in partnership with Joe Mercer, led to his drifting out of the game, where his undoubted coaching ability can no longer be utilised. He attended a match at Elland Road recently, and looked very fit for a man now in his sixties. He seems still to have plenty to offer the game, but sadly he is one of many who have been discarded by it.

I returned to Stoke to resume my Central League career and my quest for a first-team place. I had benefitted from my experience at Plymouth and finished the season as a regular reserve-team player.

The end of the season was just a few weeks away and the dreaded time for every young player was upon us. The manager was to start calling us into his office, apprentices at the end of their apprenticeships, and young professionals at the end of their contracts, and inform us whether or not we were being offered new contracts.

It is a period of terrible uncertainty for all youngsters in this position. Talk for weeks before revolves around who are favourites to be released and who are favourites to be re-engaged. One by one those in question are called into the manager's office and told of their fate. I have seen released players break down in tears, inconsolable in their disappointment. It is a devastating thing for a young player who has dreamed of becoming a footballer since early childhood to be told he has no future in the game. All his hopes and dreams and aspirations are dashed in a matter of a few minutes. There are some who, in an act of bravado, dismiss their release as being inconsequential, a minor setback to their ambitions. It is their way of handling their feelings, a more acceptable alternative to tears, but it is just as painful for them as it is for those who choose to show their emotions. My younger brother Jon suffered this same experience when he was released after two years as a professional with Stoke.

After their initial disappointment, most players in this position will try and obtain trials with clubs in lower divisions. This is achieved by a player writing a letter to the club concerned or getting help from the manager. A few will be successful, but most will drift into regular jobs, often embittered by their experience. I have met such players who, even many years later, retain a residue of bitterness, an element of pain from the period when their dreams were so cruelly crushed.

The difference between success and failure at that age is minimal. The ability of most players when contracted is generally very similar. The one thing that separates players at this stage and throughout their careers is desire. The desire to do well is the one thing that sees them improve at a greater rate than their contemporaries, and it is the one thing that will see them ultimately succeed and their contemporaries fail. I was fortunate in having a tremendous will to succeed; in the early days of my career, this was my greatest asset. It was partly due to a natural inheritance from my father and also to a longing to emulate his achievements as a player. I had the competitive relationship many sons have with their fathers. Having chosen to follow in his footsteps, the thought of failure was too painful to contemplate.

I was called into Alan Durban's office feeling satisfied with my season's achievements but not totally confident of the outcome of our meeting. My fears were unfounded and I was offered a two-year contract with twice my previous pay. Once again, haggling never occurred to me and I was only too pleased to accept these terms. I was told by the manager that I was expected to be challenging for a first-team place the following season – I had already told myself the same thing.

The 1978-79 season saw Stoke City winning promotion to the First Division after a last-match victory at Notts County. Jubilant celebrations followed and the team were rewarded with a week's holiday in Magaluf, Mallorca. I was called in to see the manager, along with Adrian Heath who went on to play for Everton and Manchester City. He is a year younger than me and had played a few games for the first team. A place on the team trip had to be filled by one or other of us as a reward for our endeavours that season. The manager was showing his sadistic side, deciding who should go by flipping a coin in our presence. Adrian called heads and we nervously watched as the manager tossed the coin into the air. To my absolute joy it came down tails – I was actually going away with the first team for the very first time. Adrian was not happy, apparently feeling he should have gone by virtue of the fact that he had made several first-team appearances. The first thing I did on arrival in Magaluf was to send Adrian a postcard. It read 'Wish you were here', and was signed by all the players – footballers can be very cruel.

Adrian was known as 'Inchy', seemingly because of his diminutive stature, although close friends hinted at another reason. I had known him from my B-team days at Stoke and we had come through the A team and reserve teams together. While I had gone to college, Inchy had signed on as an apprentice and in effect had two years' start on me. We became firm friends and enjoyed some marvellous times during our Stoke days. It is a friendship that has lasted the course and we still keep in touch to this day.

Long-standing friendships are not over common in football. From my time at Stoke I have regular contact with just two players, Inchy and Garth Crooks, who later went on to gain an FA Cup winner's medal with Tottenham Hotspur. Casual friendships are very much part and parcel of football life. The turnover of players at any club is very high and within three years, most sides will have lost or replaced a very high percentage of the team. The one-club player is almost a thing of the past. With this constant changing of faces, it is understandable why so few long-term friendships are established.

Even casual friendships, however, still involve a high degree of intimacy. Footballers often spend many long, tedious hours locked away together in hotels or travelling on coaches. Indeed nearly all players are required to have a rooming partner during their stay at hotels. This involves periods spent eating, drinking and washing together, and demands a high level of sociability amongst players. The problem of ill-matched rooming partners does arise, but not too often. Most pairs are chosen by the players themselves, and when they are selected by the manager, it is usually quite apparent to him who will get on and who will not.

The common solution to boredom is the formulation of a card school. Most teams have three or four different schools on the go at one time. They tend to play for small amounts of money, just to make things interesting. I have known certain schools play for serious money, with players gambling up to a full week's wages or more. Ironically managers, many of whom have dealt the odd hand themselves, are invariably aghast. A player can be in the position of having lost at cards and playing the ensuing match just to pay off his debts. This is a distraction not only to the player but to the team as well. A player with off-the-field problems, especially debts, inevitably runs the risk of taking them on to the field with him.

Players who are more insular occupy themselves with their favourite newspaper or book. The tabloid newspapers tend to be the preferred reading of footballers, although some do aspire to the quality journals. Most coaches are fitted with television and video facilities; a good video will break the back of the most arduous of journeys.

The following season I reported back for pre-season training full of optimism. This mood was justified when I was informed that I had been given a locker in the first-team dressing room. Up to now I had changed with the reserves and had ventured into the first-team dressing room only at reserves home matches. It was hallowed ground and only accessible during the week to those in the senior squad. For an apprentice or young professional, it was more than his life was worth to enter it without the consent of one of its occupants.

As I mentioned earlier, experience in the game usually brings with it a cynical, critical attitude with a razor-sharp sense of humour to match. The humour is unique to football and often revolves around experienced players making fun of their inexperienced colleagues, often cruelly. Inevitably a pack mentality develops in every club and any person regarded as fair game – the vulnerable, quiet type for instance – quickly finds other players joining in the ridicule. Every young player goes through this experience until he in turn acquires an attitude and sense of humour to match, when he will do to others what was done unto him. A player who is the victim of a particularly successful piece of group ridicule can often find himself labelled and open to winding up for many months to come. This especially applies in the case of nicknames, which can very easily stick, much to the embarrassment of their owners.

This was the fear that kept every young player away from the first-team dressing room. It encouraged a healthy respect for experienced professionals from the younger players. Over the years I have noticed the gradual erosion of this respect. Young players no longer view the first-team dressing room with fear and trepidation and many wander around it freely. It is, I think, to the game's detriment, but is also a reflection of many young people's attitudes in today's society.

For many years apprentices have had traditional duties, several of which are menial. Some clubs are moving away from these practices and no longer require their apprentices to continue such duties, reasoning that these youngsters should concentrate on their football education. This is a valid argument against doing such things as painting the ground and collecting rubbish after matches. Where it is not valid is in the area of boot cleaning. An apprentice assigned to the task of looking after the boots of two or three professionals has day-to-day contact with members of the first team. He asks their requirements for boot selection and length of studs. This encourages the professionals to develop an interest in the youngster, who is free to ask for advice about life on and off the field. Without this contact a chasm develops between apprentice level and first team, so much so, in fact, that an apprentice can spend two years at a club and remain unknown by name to many of the first-team members. Things have to change, but certain traditions are, I believe, essential.

The 1979–80 season started well for me and I soon began to score on a regular basis for the reserves. My objective became clear – it was to displace a big centre forward called Brendan O'Callaghan from the first team. Brendan, at six foot four, was a giant of a player who had been signed the season before from Doncaster Rovers. He had joined Stoke in the latter part of their Second Division promotion campaign and had scored within ten seconds of his debut, when coming on as substitute against Hull City. Brendan was a good team player, who provided more goals than he scored. My game was based on scoring and it was goals that would get me into the first team.

The reserve-team coach was an ex-Brighton player called Wally Gould. He was a tremendous enthusiast and played a major part in the early development of players such as myself, Adrian Heath and Paul Bracewell, who later won England honours with Everton. He had spent the latter years of his career in South Africa, and had grown accustomed to a year-round tan. This led to his daily sessions on the club's primitive sunbed. His bronzed features looked distinctly out of place alongside the pale inhabitants of the Potteries. He would occasionally fall asleep during these sessions, especially before reserve matches, and emerge a frightening shade of red. It was on these occasions that we found it extremely difficult to take his team talks seriously.

My big chance came sooner than expected. A crop of injuries in the first team had left player resources depleted for the League Cup match at Swindon Town early in October. I found my name on the team sheet for the very first time and boarded the coach for Swindon. I was in a state of panic for the whole of the day leading up to the evening game. This was my moment of truth. It was something I had longed for, but now it was about to happen I was unsure as to whether I could cope with the situation. It was one thing training with the first team, but quite another to be playing for them in a competitive match.

We arrived at the hotel prior to the match for lunch and a sleep. I hardly touched my meal and instead of sleeping I lay in my room nervously contemplating the evening's events. The hours seemed like minutes and I soon found myself on the way to the ground. We arrived, as most teams do, an hour before the match in order to begin our preparations. First on the agenda is the pitch inspection, to see if any change of studs is necessary. In my experience, most players prefer playing with a certain length of stud, and will wear these studs whatever the surface. Only severe conditions will necessitate a change.

From this point up until the kick off, every player has his own individual routine. Superstition plays a major part in these routines, to the extent that clothing and footwear will be taken off and put on in a predetermined order. This even includes any strappings, massages and warming-up exercises. A bad result would mean an adjustment to this routine, whereas a good result would guarantee its continuation. In times of stress these routines can be carried out without thought and in that respect are very beneficial. This was proving to be the case for me at Swindon as I completed my preparations in an increasing state of panic.

We ran out on to the pitch to rapturous applause. I scuffed my first two kicks of the ball in the warm-up, a feat that did nothing for my confidence. However, once the game itself began, my nerves were forgotten immediately I had played my first good ball. The game passed in a blur and my only memory was the goal I scrambled over the line. We lost the match 2–1, to go out of the competition on aggregate to a side two divisions below us, but the memory of the goal and the feelings of joy and disbelief that followed it were to remain with me. The fact that my father was at the game to witness my first senior goal made it all the more pleasing.

Any thoughts of making my First Division debut the following Saturday were soon dispelled when Brendan O'Callaghan reported fit and I was back in the reserves again. However, just under two months later, shortly before my twentieth birthday, I was selected in the squad for the trip to Southampton. I was named substitute and eagerly took my place on the bench, hoping for an introduction to First Division football. It came twenty minutes from the end of play as Stoke were losing. I positively raced on to the pitch, realising another dream – to play in the First Division.

Within minutes my vision of life at the top was somewhat tarnished. I had challenged for the ball with a Southampton player, Steve Williams, and managed to come out on top. I passed the ball to a colleague and as I turned away, Williams reacted in a way I found hard to comprehend – whether intentionally or not, he spat in my face. Up until that moment he had been someone I had respected for his obvious potential as a player. Any respect for him as a person was wiped away, along with the spittle on my face.

It was back to the reserves again for six weeks until I made another appearance in the number twelve shirt, going down this time at Ipswich. The following match I was given my full debut, at home against Bristol City. This time I had control of my nerves and performed well. The following week I scored at Crystal

Palace, and by the end of the season had made a total of fourteen appearances.

Stoke was an ideal club for any youngster to make his mark. It was a small, unambitious set-up with a relaxed family atmosphere. First Division survival was the main objective and there seemed to be no real desire to achieve anything else, especially, it appeared, at boardroom level.

The club had a long-standing reputation for recruiting established professionals nearing the end of their careers. The practice began under Tony Waddington's managership when he signed the forty-six-year-old Stanley Matthews. Players such as goalkeeper Roger Jones, Ray Evans (ex-Tottenham), Mike Doyle (ex-Manchester City) and Viv Busby (ex-Fulham) all finished their First Division careers whilst I was at Stoke. The club had a mixture of the latter type of player, local youngsters and players bought from clubs in the lower leagues. A few years earlier, Mr Waddington had bought the likes of Alan Hudson and Peter Shilton but the financial situation no longer justified bids for established internationals. It seemed that those running the club were happy with this status. There was never an impetus to generate the level of income needed to compete at the highest level. This was something that constantly frustrated the supporters and the club's more ambitious players. Nevertheless Stoke did at least maintain First Division status, something they long for at the present time.

The following season, I became a first-team regular and finished the campaign with seventeen goals. The highlight of this season was my second hat trick, scored at Elland Road, of all places, in our 3–1 victory over Leeds United. Little did I imagine that I would repeat this feat many years later in the colours of Leeds.

On one of my first trips with the first-team squad, I and three colleagues showed just how naive young professionals can be. The club were in Athens to play the Greek side Panathinaikos. I was one of four younger members of the first-team squad who had decided to visit the Acropolis. We could see it quite clearly from our hotel, but once we were fighting our way through the bustle of Athens, we were far from sure of our whereabouts. We were definitely lost, a fact that must have been all too apparent to the owner of a seedy bar, who was standing on a street corner.

He approached us and asked, in very impressive English, what was wrong. 'We're trying to find the Acropolis,' we muttered.

'Oh,' he replied. 'You're out of luck today – the Acropolis is closed.' 'Really?' was our feeble response. 'Yes, why don't you come into my bar for a drink instead?' It would have been the first time the Acropolis had been closed since its completion thousands of years ago, but we believed him and went into his bar, where we ordered four beers and sat back to enjoy them. To our amazement, four scantily dressed women appeared from nowhere and asked if we were going to buy them a drink. We were like lambs to the slaughter. As we ordered their drinks, the women sat themselves down on our knees. It seemed to be our lucky day. It was only when their hands disappeared down our trousers that we realised they were on the game. We quickly asked for the bill. To our horror, we were being asked to pay the equivalent of £40 for eight drinks. We thought about leaving without paying, but were dissuaded from doing this when a giant of a Greek appeared at the doorway. To make matters worse, we related the story to the rest of the players, who made us squirm in embarrassment for many weeks afterwards.

Wally Gould had become first-team coach, and he proved a great help to players such as Peter Fox, Paul Bracewell, Adrian Heath and myself, who had all risen from reserve level to first team along with him. Adrian and I had a great rapport with Wally, who would do anything for us. We even persuaded him that the current first-team strip of red and white stripes with a collared shirt should be changed. We argued that a broader stripe along with a V-neck shirt would look far better – similar to the Argentinian national team strip. Wally duly ordered the strip from manufacturers Umbro without informing anybody of his intentions to actually use it for League matches. We wore the new strip for three League matches before uproar, from supporters wanting to buy the new strip, and Umbro who could not supply it, caused the club to withdraw the new and reintroduce the old.

This story emphasises the relaxed attitude of nearly everyone connected with the club. It extended to off-the-field activities as well. The pub was a regular meeting place for players after training early in the week. These lunchtime sessions would often drift into the afternoon and early evening. In those days it was not regarded as detrimental to the performance on the pitch. In fact many coaches at the time would encourage youngsters to have a good drink early in the week and sweat it out in training the following day. They might not have been so happy had they known the extent of our intake. The idea of 'sweating out' was popular at the time; it was believed to rid the body of any abuse received the previous night. Players would often train wearing black dustbin liners, their arms and legs protruding at the corners, in a desperate attempt to sweat.

Our ignorance about preparation also extended to diet. Large steaks were believed to be the essential food of top footballers. It was also thought that any carbohydrates such as potatoes and bread should be severely rationed. Many players would consume steaks at every opportunity. Some would even eat fillet steak as a pre-match meal, two and a half hours before a game. They would consume negligible amounts of bread and potatoes, and pasta was not even contemplated. It is amazing how these players managed to perform at all.

During the fourteen years I have been in the game at professional level, I have seen a dramatic change in attitudes to food, drink and general preparation for matches.

When I first began my career, the heavy-drinking professional footballer was quite common. In fact, experienced players of this ilk were often regarded as role models to be emulated by youngsters starting out on their careers. Over the years this attitude has gradually changed and in recent times the number of heavy drinkers has greatly decreased. This especially applies to those performing at the top levels of the game, i.e., Premier League and international players. The game has changed beyond all recognition in terms of physical and mental awareness. The pressures placed upon the modern footballer simply mean that excessive drinkers are unable to compete at the top for any length of time. Public and media awareness is now at such a high level that exposure of such vices is a distinct possibility.

A revolution in dietary requirements has also taken place. The myth of the large, rare steak has now been dispelled for ever. A low-protein, high-carbohydrate diet is generally accepted as being beneficial to physical performance. Small portions of protein, such as low-fat red meat, chicken and fish, are coupled with high doses of carbohydrates such as bread, potatoes and especially pasta. Pasta is generally regarded as being particularly beneficial and many clubs actively encourage players to consume it in the forty-eight hours before a match. A generous intake of vegetables is also known to be highly advantageous, along with copious amounts of fluids, preferably water. Fluid replacement has been proven vital in fighting off a reduction in performance level. The importance of avoiding dehydration has been realised only in the last few years.

These principles have been adhered to by athletes and tennis players from the early eighties onwards. Dr Robert Haas first expanded on these theories in his book *Eat to Win*, which I read with great interest in the mid-eighties. English football has many exemplary qualities, but innovation is not one of them. As always, change in the English game has happened slowly and these principles have only recently begun to be accepted.

Players today are more enlightened than they ever have been and are continually looking for ways to improve their performance in an increasingly competitive game. Massage, biokinetics, stretching, vitamins and mineral supplements are just some of the things being used in the search for excellence. Professional masseurs have long been employed by every Continental club. It is amazing that only recently have players here begun to appreciate the benefits of massage. We are now seeing players performing at the very top whilst in their mid-thirties, and even beyond. In many cases they are playing the best football of their careers – Gordon Strachan of Leeds and Ray Wilkins of Queen's Park Rangers are just two examples. It is no coincidence that players of this type are exponents of the innovations discussed above. Not only can they improve performance level for any age group, they can also extend the length of a footballer's career.

The 1980–81 season, although finishing on a high note personally, was tinged with sadness. Sammy Irvine, Stoke's Scottish midfield player, had been forced to retire in his mid-twenties. Sammy had been involved in a horrendous car crash the previous season. His Triumph TR7 had collided head-on with a tree. Sammy was fortunate to survive; he was in a coma for several days, suffering from serious head injuries. During the 1980–81 season he had tried in vain to make a recovery in the reserves, even though his movement was restricted. His co-ordination never recovered sufficiently for him to regain his former mobility and he reluctantly decided to retire.

This was tragic enough for any player, but it seemed more so in Sammy's case. He was an extremely popular player, with a wicked sense of humour. A pop record of the time was Dawn's 'Tie a Yellow Ribbon Round the Old Oak Tree', and Sammy was often heard singing his own version, 'Tie a TR7 Round the Old Oak

Tree'. With anybody else it would have been in extremely bad taste, but with Sammy, you just had to laugh. His early departure was a sad loss to the game.

The end of the season brought the customary club tour. This year we were going to Barbados and everybody wanted to get on the trip, directors and players alike. End-of-season trips are generally an excuse for everybody to let their hair down and enjoy each other's company without the pressure of competitive matches.

The relaxation generally starts at the airport and continues well into the flight. This trip was no exception and after a few hours on board, generous amounts of drink had made most of our party as relaxed as they could be. One particular passenger had spent a lot of time trying to smoothtalk a couple of Scandinavian girls. He was obviously getting nowhere fast, much to his frustration. In his drunken state, he must have decided that if he could not get his way fairly, he would get it any way he could. His solution was to slip sleeping tablets into the girls' drinks. They were soon in a blissful sleep and at the man's mercy. He decided upon a quick grope with each girl and then left them to sleep it off. The behaviour, on tours abroad, on occasion leaves a lot to be desired. Even directors, who are often regarded as the ones to uphold the moral values at any club and to set the right example, do not always behave well.

While most married and attached footballers tread the straight and narrow away from home, that generally cannot be said for single players. They exercise what they believe is their right to do whatever they want with whoever they want. In the somewhat male chauvinistic world of football, single players especially treat women with scant regard. For many, they are there to be used and abused at every opportunity. It is something that happens in most walks of life, although it tends to be more exaggerated in the world of football. Single footballers have a great attraction for the opposite sex, and opportunities are plentiful. Who could blame any hot-blooded single male for taking full advantage of this situation?

Footballers have few equals as gossipmongers and any conquest is quickly common knowledge. News travels quickly on the dressing-room grapevine, and of course every storyteller adds his own little embellishment. The better stories even pass from club to club, although often grossly distorted from their original form. Much of this gossiping occurs during the many tedious hours spent travelling or staying in hotels.

During our stay in Barbados we lived in villas with six players sharing each one. Our villa was mainly composed of single players who were inclined to have house guests from time to time. One such guest was a buxom Welsh lass from the Rhondda Valley. She had kept pace with her partner, pint for pint, for the whole evening. This punishing session had taken its toll and she now lay in bed in a near comatose state.

On our return to the villa, we were ushered into the bedroom to witness her sorry state. Gentlemen would then have left, but we were all in a very merry condition, and we saw the chance for a bit of fun. The youngest member of our party was given a full anatomy lesson, much to his embarrassment. A cocktail stirrer was used to point out various features of the poor girl's naked body. This finished, the unfortunate victim was then turned over, so that her rear was in full view of everybody. It was her misfortune that a pen was handily placed on the bedside table. Five minutes later her backside was adorned with smiley faces and signatures. Each signature had an accompanying message thanking her for the favours she had supposedly bestowed on one and all. Not an inch of flesh was spared.

The following morning she awoke, completely unaware of the previous night's events and the personalised artwork inscribed on her rear. She donned her bikini and thanked her partner for a pleasant evening. It was late morning and she was going straight down to the beach to meet her friends. Little did she know she was about to endure one of the most embarrassing moments of her life.

Life was one long quest for laughs and good times. We never burdened ourselves with questions of morality, no matter how insensitive or immature our actions were. Although footballers become very worldly at a comparatively early age, their sense of responsibility and maturity develops at a somewhat slower pace. They travel the world and visit places many people never see in a lifetime. All this is done in the cosseted environment of the football club. In many ways it acts as a cocoon against the harsh realities of most people's lives. A footballer's existence is structured by the club to such an extent that many players become dependent on this way of life. This structuring is especially evident on away trips when times of eating, sleeping, working and recreation are all decided for you by the club.

Most clubs attempt to remove all burdens of worry, so enabling players to concentrate solely on football. It is true that a player with problems in his life will invariably find them affecting his game, and in this respect the club's attitude is definitely helpful. At the same time, the club is not encouraging young men to take responsibility for their own lives. No player in his teens or early twenties can really envisage his playing days coming to an end. It seems that this wonderful life within football must go on forever. I certainly felt that way. I knew that most players finished playing in their early or mid-thirties, but it was surely impossible that I too would reach this stage one day. As the years roll by, the end gradually becomes more of a reality. I now view my remaining years as ones to be cherished. I no longer remain oblivious to the inevitable; life outside football has to be contemplated.

At the time of our trip to Barbados, Alan Durban was considering life away from Stoke City. He had been offered the chance to manage Sunderland, the so-called 'Sleeping Giants'. Stoke had finished the season in a mid-table position. Alan realised this was as far as he could take the team without upsetting the board of directors, who were obviously happy with things as they were. There seemed a lack of ambition amongst those running the club, a fact that was only too apparent to the players as well. Stoke had come to be regarded as a stepping stone to greater things, for managers and players alike.

Alan's mistake was to regard Sunderland as a suitable vehicle for his undoubted managerial talents. A club that has been a sleeping giant for as long as Sunderland had clearly has deep-rooted problems. Alan was later to wish he had examined these problems more closely, as were many managers over the years, both before and after his reign.

I had the greatest respect for Alan as a boss. He undoubtedly helped me enormously in my formative years in the game, as he did other youngsters who have gone on to distinguished careers – Adrian Heath, Paul Bracewell and Steve Bould (who was a reserve player during my time at Stoke), to name just a few. Alan had played for many years under Brian Clough and had formulated his style of management during this time. He was a likeable Welshman who was a strict disciplinarian but generous to players who performed for him. He seemed destined for a long and successful career; unfortunately, this was not to be.

An amicable parting was agreed with Stoke, and Alan left for Sunderland, recommending Shrewsbury manager Richie Barker for the vacant manager's job. The board accepted his recommendation and duly implemented it. It soon became apparent that Richie was going to do things his way. An early casualty of the new regime was first-team coach Wally Gould, who was dismissed. It was sad to see Wally go after three happy years with him. He was unable to get back into the game and became a painter and decorator in the Stoke area, still topping up his year-round tan, I've no doubt.

Many hours were spent on the training ground rehearsing new team patterns in readiness for the new season. We began well, with two victories for the team, and three goals for myself. After our bright start, however, the season gradually deteriorated. Halfway through the season, as our results became poorer, Adrian Heath, my partner in crime, was sold to Everton, by now managed by Howard Kendall. It seemed the club were willing to sell their best players, and I became increasingly agitated. This resulted in a string of bust-ups with the manager over the remaining matches, culminating with his vowing that I would never play for the club again after a home defeat by Notts County, three matches from the end of the season.

The following game, a visit to Manchester United, I was relegated to substitute. We lost, and went into our final match needing a victory to retain our First Division status. The remaining relegation place rested between ourselves and Leeds United. Victory against West Bromwich Albion in our final match would send Leeds to the Second Division. Two nights earlier, Leeds had lost their last game – also against Albion – and some of their supporters had rioted after the match.

The result at the Victoria Ground was never in doubt and we won comfortably, 3–0. It was ironic that I should score two goals and doom my future club to eight long years in the Second Division. In fact I was to join Leeds as that eight-year sentence was finishing, during their Second Division promotion campaign. This time my goals helped to return Leeds to their rightful place among the elite. By a strange quirk of fate, I was able to undo the harm I had inflicted upon them all those years ago.

My contract with Stoke was nearing its end and I awaited an offer of re-engagement. The club, in keeping with their overall unambitious attitude, made me a paltry offer. This reinforced my dissatisfaction with life at Stoke and I decided it was time to leave. My great friend Adrian Heath had gone on to bigger and better things at Everton and I was now determined to follow suit.

It was during this year that the freedom of contract rule was brought into force. Players at the end of their contracts were now free to sign for another club if a transfer fee could be agreed. If a fee could not be resolved, the matter went to a tribunal where the transfer fee of a player was decided by an independent panel. Previously players had been unable to move if the selling club did not receive the asking price; if the fee was not met, the player remained at the club.

I reported for pre-season training a Stoke player, but only just. I was now on a week-to-week contract and unsure of my future. Goalkeeper Eric McManus and defender Alan Dodd were in the same position. After an initial period of training with the rest of the players, we were all informed by Richie Barker that we were not allowed to continue doing so. We were banished to another part of the training ground to train alone. There is a limit to what can be achieved in training with only two other players, and after several tedious days of this routine, we decided to train elsewhere.

Contact was made with arch-rivals Port Vale, my father's old club, and manager John McGrath kindly allowed us to train with his squad. It was an embarrassing situation for Stoke and one I am sure that Port Vale relished. Jimmy Greenhoff, who had been a hero of mine during his playing days with Stoke, was now a player at Port Vale. Another member of the playing staff was a young Mark Chamberlain, later to play for England and link up with me at Sheffield Wednesday.

My spell with Vale did not last long. Three days later I was given a message by John McGrath; I was to contact a reporter called John Maddock who worked for the *People*. John was a friend of my father's and could be trusted. I called him and was told to get in touch with Arsenal manager Terry Neill for a chat. I could not believe what I was hearing, but nervously dialled the number I had been given by John. Terry Neill answered the phone and asked if I would travel south to discuss a possible move. I eagerly agreed and told him I would be in London later that day.

·4·

Bright lights, hard times

The idea of a night on the Six Towns had lost its appeal. After seventeen years of living in Stoke-on-Trent, I wanted London. Now, it seemed, Arsenal wanted me.

My eagerness must have been only too apparent to everybody at Highbury. Contractual discussions were conducted in a take-it-or-leave-it fashion. They knew only too well that I was so anxious to play for Arsenal that I was bound to sign.

Arsenal have been notorious for many years for luring players on the strength of the tradition and history of the club. After being guided around the famous marble hallway and shown the impressive trophy cabinet, I was told what a great club Arsenal were and that this was an opportunity I could not refuse. Like a lamb to the slaughter, I accepted everything put before me and questioned nothing.

It was not a bad deal, but I could have done a lot better. In those days, that flourishing species the agent was in the embryonic stage. Agents who are responsible and have the best interests of the player at heart are, I believe, good for the game and have done much to better players' earning power. I was a naive twenty-two-year-old and would have benefitted greatly from having such an operator at my side.

My discussions were conducted with Terry Neill and company secretary Ken Friar, who is now managing director. Like a police double act – the tough guy and his more compassionate partner – the two went through a routine they must have perfected over many such transfers. I came out of the talks feeling manipulated and having missed an opportunity to negotiate a much better deal. My advice to any professional, young or old, in any contractual discussions would be to seek the assistance of a responsible adviser. The contract was to be signed the following day. I was then driven to the West Park Lodge in Hadley Wood, a charming, isolated hotel on the outskirts of London.

I called my father, who had been unaware of the day's events. He was surprised to learn that I was in London and on the brink of signing for Arsenal, and advised me to be patient and delay signing in order to consider any other options. He had reservations about my suitability for their style of play, and the London environment. I thanked him for his advice, but told him I intended to sign. It was pointless him talking to me; I was headstrong and impatient and had already made my decision.

Terry Neill arrived at the hotel that evening and informed me that Stoke manager Richie Barker was trying to contact me. He said that Barker was making one final attempt to keep me at Stoke, and that I shouldn't call him because of this. I naively believed him and decided not to make contact. Shortly after I had put pen to paper, I was informed that Richie Barker had been attempting to get in touch with me for an entirely different reason. He had agreed on a transfer fee for me with Ron Atkinson, then manager of Manchester United, and wanted to know if I was interested in a move there. At the very least, I would have had talks there and may have even signed. In many ways a move to Manchester would have been just as appealing as one to London.

I felt completely hollow on hearing this news. I felt as though I had been cheated twice – once over my contract and now over a possible move to Manchester United. In many ways my impatience, and naivety, had cost me dear, but I also felt I had been dealt with in a less than honest way. It was not the best of starts with my new club, and the situation deteriorated even further shortly afterwards.

Arsenal and Stoke had been unable to agree a fee for my transfer and so it was to go before a tribunal who would decide the exact figure. Stoke were demanding £750,000 and Arsenal were offering £250,000, a large discrepancy indeed. Stoke were using a bartering technique, demanding a high price, but in reality happy to accept a lower one, whereas Arsenal were making an honest bid and expecting to pay no more than £350,000.

All parties were summoned before the tribunal, which consisted mainly of Football League bureaucrats, at a London hotel, and were asked to give reasons for their valuations. I was asked banal questions about why I wanted to leave Stoke, and why I wanted to join Arsenal. It seemed I was there as a procedural formality.

After a short private deliberation, the panel emerged to give their decision. The fee was set at £500,000. The reactions of the two clubs were most distinct. The officials from Stoke left with broad smiles, whereas those from Arsenal could not hide their shock. I looked at Terry Neill's face and his disappointment was transparent. Not a word was said to me and I was left sitting there feeling totally inadequate. The manager was even quoted in the next day's newspapers as being very unhappy with the valuation. I was getting the distinct impression that the club were far from happy with my presence at Highbury, and that was before I had even kicked a ball. My dream move was already beginning to turn a little sour.

Life in London was not how I had imagined it either. As part of the move, it was agreed that I should stay in a hotel for three months at Arsenal's expense, a thing that is normal practice at most clubs. The hotel I was staying in was ideal for a weekend break, but hardly suitable for a young footballer on his own. It was in fact extremely quiet and hardly the exciting lifestyle I had been expecting. I knew very few people in London, and the prospect of this situation improving seemed somewhat remote. The former Nottingham Forest and England striker Tony Woodcock and his family were also staying in the hotel. Tony had signed from Cologne shortly before my arrival and was in the process of searching for a house. The peaceful atmosphere of the hotel suited Tony's requirements much more than it did mine.

A hotel is never an ideal place to live on a permanent basis, with or without a family. The first week is something of a novelty, but life soon becomes restrictive and depressing. At first it is extremely enjoyable eating rich food in a restaurant, but after a while you begin to yearn for simple food in the relaxed surroundings of your own home. In the end, the hotel room becomes a luxurious bedsit and the hotel staff invaders of your privacy.

I joined Arsenal halfway through their pre-season training, with about three weeks left until the first game of the new season. I had inevitably missed a lot of fitness training due to Richie Barker's refusal to allow me to train with the other players at Stoke. I was well aware of this fact, but was hoping I could catch up on lost fitness during the following three weeks.

A few days after signing I left with the team for a short trip to Egypt. We were to play a match in Alexandria and return home the following day. The match was played in almost unbearable heat. One of the players, Stewart Robson, suffered from heat exhaustion. I made a brief appearance as substitute as the team scraped a draw.

After the game we returned to Cairo ready for the flight home the following morning. We arrived in Cairo in the evening and checked into our hotel, from where the club had organised transport for any player wishing to go and see the Sphinx and the Great Pyramids. It was an opportunity that could not be turned down, or so I thought. Four players boarded the coach for this trip. Those remaining formed card schools or watched television.

A reluctance to make an effort to see anything of the places they are visiting is not peculiar to Arsenal. Over the years I have found this attitude to be common among many players. Footballers visit many exotic and far-flung locations during their travels. On many occasions preparation for matches does not allow for sightseeing and exploration, yet even when it does, I have known players prefer the facilities of the hotel rather than explore places they may never have the chance to see again. I am reminded of the television documentary of West Bromwich Albion's historic tour of China in the late seventies. One of the few players who took up the chance to see the Great Wall was asked for his impressions. 'See one wall,' he replied, 'and you've seen them all.'

We arrived at the site of the Sphinx in total darkness, minutes before sunrise. As the sun came up directly behind one of the Wonders of the World, revealing its features a little at a time, I realised it was an experience I would not forget.

As the season approached I became increasingly worried about my readiness for the fray. Our final pre-season friendly was against Chelsea, a game we won comfortably. I had managed to score, but felt some way off my best. I had a quiet word with Don Howe, the coach, and told him about my fears. Don reassured me and told me not to worry.

By one of these strange quirks of fate that football is always conjuring, my League debut for Arsenal was to be against my previous club, Stoke, at the Victoria Ground. I had left Stoke with a certain amount of acrimony and I knew a warm reception awaited me. I not only had to contend with a nerve-racking debut, but also ill feelings from the team I was playing and the Stoke crowd. My price tag was now beginning to weigh very heavily indeed. It had not worried me during the previous three weeks, but now the moment of truth was approaching I suddenly felt extremely uncomfortable with it.

I had been bought as a replacement for Frank Stapleton, who had moved to Manchester United. Frank was a cultured forward who fitted neatly into Arsenal's system of slow build-up play. He had also been a firm crowd favourite and would be a hard act to follow. Supporters were expecting a carbon-copy replacement, and I knew only too well I was anything but that.

I was no more than a promising young centre forward who had more than a few rough edges. I had been used at Stoke as an out-and-out target man, mainly aerial. Their game had been very direct and much of my work was done in the opposition's penalty area. Now I was being asked to play a totally foreign game. I was expected to get involved in intricate build-up play as well as to score goals. In time, I have no doubt, I could have learnt to adapt, but time was something I did not have. The size of my fee dictated that I should play straight away, instead of learning the system at reserve-team level, as I might have done at a club like Liverpool.

Confidence is everything in football; without it a player has nothing. As I went to bed in our hotel on the eve of my debut, I was feeling anything but confident. I had the worst night's sleep I have ever experienced and rose the following morning feeling totally exhausted. This only added to my poor frame of mind. I had virtually convinced myself that I was bound to perform badly later that day.

As expected, a large welcoming party was waiting to greet me at the Victoria Ground. As I disembarked from the coach, I was met by a crescendo of booing – the traitor had returned. I felt very strange as I entered the away team dressing room for the first time in over three years; it was almost surreal.

This feeling followed me on to the pitch where I had a hugely disappointing game. We lost 2–1 and I trundled off the pitch both depressed and embarrassed. I knew many people were relishing the prospect of my falling flat on my face, and that was exactly what I had done. It seemed there was only one thing to do – drown my sorrows. Unfortunately, I had arranged to stay in Stoke for the weekend, something I was bitterly regretting. It was the last place I wanted to be after the day's events.

All footballers are affected by defeat and bad performances. Younger players tend to take things very much to heart. The game is run over in the mind time and time again, in a futile attempt to eradicate errors already made. The older professional is more likely to take things in his stride and subscribe to the philosophical view that it is the next game that counts. Defeat and bad performances are an inevitable part of football and if they are merely occasional hiccups, they must be treated as such. But I was young, and that evening I was very depressed. I could not see ahead to the next game; all I could do was wallow in my disappointment.

Three days later I made my home debut against Norwich. It was a tight game, with the score at 1–1 with minutes to play. A cross came over to the far post, and I rose and planted a firm header into the goal. I exploded with joy at the prospect of having scored the winning goal. My elation was short-lived – the referee blew for an infringement that only he had seen. I was devastated. It seemed nothing would go right. That goal would have been a lifeline for me. It would have given me a much-needed boost. Instead I found my confidence was slowly draining away.

The following match was at home to Liverpool and was televised for BBC's *Match of the Day*. We were beaten 2–0 in front of a frustrated crowd of 36,000. One particular clip of action was shown later that evening, much to my embarrassment. The ball was squared to me about eight yards out, with the goal at my mercy. I took a wild kick at the ball, but missed it completely, much to the derision of the home supporters. The following pictures said it all, as I was shown rigid with tension, wishing the ground would swallow me up. Yet I am indebted to the BBC for replaying that embarrassing moment, even today. I look at the player on the screen and it seems like a different person; I can barely recognise myself. It is strange how people – those at the BBC included – still associate me with my troubled times at Arsenal, even though they occurred a decade ago.

The following game at Brighton brought yet another defeat, to make it three in the first four matches, and one draw besides – hardly an encouraging start. By this time, some of the Arsenal players had decided I was not their sort of player. Arsenal had a tradition for deft touch play, twinned with a slow build-up. This was definitely not suited to my direct and unsophisticated type of football. Instead of toleration, I was in many ways given the cold-shoulder treatment and looked down upon by a certain few.

I had been warned by George Wood, our amiable Scottish goalkeeper, about the cliquish atmosphere that existed at Highbury, and it now seemed there were basically two groups within the team –

the international set, and those who were non-internationals, with one or two exceptions. I sensed a certain amount of snobbery, which extended to off-the-field socialising. This included certain players wining and dining at a particular director's house on a regular basis. It was an atmosphere unconducive to a winning team and one I found very different from my years at Stoke. The general attitude of people in the capital also sharply contrasted with those from the Potteries. It seemed people had little time for each other as they went about their lives in frenetic fashion. Rudeness and insensitivity prevailed, things which made my experience seem all the worse.

The following game at Coventry enabled us to secure our first win at the fifth attempt, with a 2–0 scoreline. I even managed to score my first goal for the club, something I celebrated by running to the dead-ball line with my arms aloft. I turned around expecting to see half a dozen team-mates sharing my joy, only to find just one at my side. It was something that did not pass unnoticed by friends at the game.

Scoring my debut goal had provided a much-needed boost to my morale, so much so that I found myself actually looking forward to the next match. This was a UEFA Cup tie in Moscow against Spartak, a team that contained several members of the Soviet national team – goalkeeper Rinat Daseyev included. In a match played in the Olympic Stadium, before 70,000 spectators, we led 2–0, only to finish 3–2 losers. I scored our opening goal and gave my best performance in an Arsenal shirt.

It seemed that things were beginning to go right. A win and a draw in the League followed, then we were to play the home leg of the UEFA Cup tie. Any good coming from the previous four matches faded into insignificance as Spartak humiliated us 5–2. I was on the scoresheet again, although I took little satisfaction from it. A 3–2 defeat at home to West Ham ensued, and although I had scored three goals in six matches, I found myself off the team sheet for the following game.

After a terrible start to my career at Highbury, I had resigned myself to expect the worst. Hope had returned to me, however, during a four-game period when I had started to resemble something of the player I had been. I had been given ten matches to prove myself, and had failed. At a club like Stoke, I would undoubtedly have been given much longer, but I was at Arsenal, where pressures and expectations were so much greater.

There was no time for a rookie centre forward to learn his trade in the first team. Success was an immediate requirement and Terry Neill knew that only too well. He was a man under intense strain, a situation that was apparent even to me. Several years later I spoke to Terry about my traumatic period at Highbury and he told me he should have done more to help me during those difficult days. Maybe he could have done, but pressure on a person's job can make anybody behave in strange and mysterious ways. I was one of just many problems begging to be solved.

There was also little doubt that various members of the team viewed me with contempt. Their game was based on deftness of touch and subtlety, whereas mine was based on physical presence and commitment. The amalgamation of all these qualities could have provided the team with much greater potential, but because of the absolute refusal of some players to accommodate my differing qualities, this was never to be. It is ironic that one of the reasons for Arsenal's recent success has been George Graham's ability to instil these qualities in the present team. I have no doubt that I would have fared much better under his management than I did under Terry Neill's. Skill and artistry are essential attributes for any successful team to possess, but only if they are married to honesty and commitment. I have no doubt that some of those looking down their noses at me were lacking in the latter qualities.

My omission from the team was a severe blow to me, even in my troubled circumstances. I had been an automatic first-team choice for two years at Stoke and was not used to the humbling experience of being dropped. Two years is indeed a long time in football, where fortunes fluctuate on a weekly basis. I had become conditioned to being a permanent member of the team, and the realisation of my exclusion was hard to take in. Even though I had endured an extremely disappointing start at my new club, I fully expected my presence in the team to continue.

The initial feeling of despondency at being dropped is followed by one of anger, usually directed towards the manager. If this anger is not channelled towards the man responsible it is often an unfortunate friend or member of the family who takes the brunt of it. Younger players will often sulk, whereas the older professional will have probably experienced the feeling on one or more occasions previously, and will be able to handle it in a more mature way. Whatever the age and whatever the circumstances, though, it always hurts. Footballers are a proud breed by the very nature of the job. It is a very public profession where success and failure are highlighted equally. The highs are there for everyone to see, a fact that makes them feel even better, whereas the lows are just as obvious and even more painful because of it.

Once out of the first team you often find your treatment is not quite as it was before. The verbal agreement that I should be allowed to stay in the hotel for the usual three months was amazingly forgotten. I was asked by Terry Neill to vacate my room immediately, even though I had only been there for eight weeks. I argued that I understood that the agreement had been for three months, but my pleas fell on deaf ears. I started to look for alternative accommodation. Looking back I might have expected the club to help me in my search for a roof over my head, but that was obviously asking far too much. I could barely find my way from the hotel to the stadium; I did not have a clue where I should start to look for property.

John Hawley had moved from Sunderland to Arsenal the previous season and had been through a similar experience to mine. A successful striker with Sunderland and Leeds, he now found himself languishing in the reserves. He had been given the opportunity to rent a club house, one of two adjacent to each other. He informed me that the other was vacant, though bare of carpets or furniture – the club would surely make it habitable for my use.

I approached the manager with my request. He responded by agreeing that I could use the house, but although I would be living in it for only a short time, I would have to carpet and furnish it myself. When a club wants to sign a player, nothing is too much trouble – they cannot do enough for him. When he has signed and is not meeting expectations, the bare minimum of help can usually be expected.

The house was a dismal modern terraced property in an unattractive part of Southgate. I furnished it sparsely and laid cheap carpet in the bare minimum of rooms; I was damned if I was going to carpet the whole house for the benefit of the club. I was sitting there one night, on my own, eating a cold dinner off my lap (I had no cooker) when the thought suddenly struck me – if you are going to have a bad time, there cannot be a worse place to have it than London. I had come to the capital expecting fame and fortune. They seemed light years away from me now. Little did I know this was not the lowest ebb; it was to get far worse.

I commenced my long and distinguished career with the reserves in the Football Combination. This was interspersed with regular slots on the first-team substitutes' bench. I even managed to come on and score on a couple of occasions, and when injuries dictated I would sometimes get a full game.

This pattern continued into the New Year. I had recently scored for the first team when coming on as a substitute and had hoped for a run in the team. I was training very hard in the hope that I could claim my place back, but for many weeks I had been getting severe pains in my left knee when I would be unable to train until the discomfort disappeared. It had even been suggested by the coaching staff that I was imagining the problem, something which obviously annoyed me. I had always prided myself on my honesty and now it was being questioned. Before long, I was vindicated in the worst possible way. One day in training I was struck by an agonising pain in my knee. The joint seized up and I collapsed to the ground. I was carried back to the dressing room, unable to straighten my leg further than forty-five degrees.

I was taken to a specialist who diagnosed a torn cartilage. I was admitted to hospital immediately and operated on the following morning. I awoke from surgery to find my left leg in plaster from my thigh to my ankle. The offending piece of cartilage had been removed and I now faced four weeks in plaster, followed by a period of rehabilitation.

Things have changed drastically in recent times. The advent of keyhole surgery has meant that immobilisation of the joint in plaster is no longer necessary. The joint can be used almost immediately and therefore no muscle wastage occurs and no rehabilitation is needed. In many cases players can be back playing within two to three weeks, a dramatic improvement on my recovery period of eight weeks. When my plaster was removed I was amazed by the wastage that had occurred in my leg muscles. The comparison with my undamaged leg provided a startling contrast. It was a long, hard journey back to full fitness and my return to competitive matches.

It had been two and a half months since my injury and I had just started playing for the reserve team again. It was one evening around that time, in late March, that I received a devastating phone call. I answered the phone to find my sister, Denise, on the other end, obviously in distress, and unable to speak. A family friend came on the line and broke the news of my father's death. He had been playing five-a-side football, as he did most weeks, when he suddenly collapsed and died of a massive heart attack. He was only forty-nine and a fitness fanatic. He carried no surplus weight, did not smoke, and rarely drank alcohol. He had complained of chest pains during his twice-weekly cross-country runs, but thought them to be a sign of lack of fitness. When they persisted he consulted a specialist and was tested for heart defects. None of the tests showed any problems and he returned to his previous lifestyle.

I sat in the dismal surroundings of the club house, unable to absorb the news I had received. I have never felt as alone as I did that night. When I finally managed to sleep, I kept waking, hoping I had experienced a nightmare. The following morning I returned home to my family.

I had just started to get to know my father as a friend, rather than as a son, and he had become a confidant, especially during my ill-fated days at Arsenal. He had never wanted me to go to London, and I was now wishing I had heeded his advice. I realised I had been impetuous and was now paying the price.

My father had also paid the price. He had been out of professional football for about two years, unable to get another job in the game. He had only ever known the world of football, as a player, coach and manager over a period of thirty years. His time in the game had seen him earn very little money and in his need to pay the bills he had taken a job as a sports company representative. He had spent the majority of his job under great stress behind the wheel of his company car. After spending his life out in the open, he was now confined to a car for most of the week, and I have few doubts that this change in lifestyle resulted in his death. The mind is all-powerful and my father had been desperately unhappy for quite some time.

I returned to London after the funeral and attempted to resurrect my faltering career. Within three weeks I found myself as substitute for the first team, and the following game I was selected for the team – the first time in nearly four months. It was an away match at Norwich and a chance to re-establish myself. I began well and felt full of confidence. It was as though my long absence had given me a fresh start, after all my troubles.

How wrong I was. Some things are not meant to be, and shortly afterwards I found myself being led from the field, blood gushing from my nose. A collision of heads with Norwich's John Deehan had resulted in a severe fracture of my nose. It was quite literally spread across my face, with all the accompanying loss of blood this entails. That evening I found myself again in hospital, undergoing yet another operation, this time to realign my nose. It was set in plaster and my season was finished. I was as low as I could get. There was surely only one way left to go – or was there? I was not convinced.

I look back at my first season with Arsenal and realise what a horrendous period it was for me. If anything could go wrong, it did, and with monotonous regularity. Bad form, injuries and the loss of my father all combined to make it the worst year of my life. I hope I never have to endure such a time again. Towards the end of this spell I had grown accustomed to my bad luck and expected nothing else. Each new mishap came as no surprise. Success and good fortune can become habitual, as can failure and misfortune. The latter had become a habit of mine.

The summer break gave me a chance to forget my problems, if only for a while. I had remained in close contact with my old friend Adrian Heath, and we decided to go on holiday together. Adrian was enjoying great success at Everton, during their purple period of League championship and FA Cup successes. These were the things I had envisaged winning at Arsenal. Our contrast in fortunes was perfectly emphasised during our time away. Adrian was constantly recognised and in great demand for his autograph. I was invariably ignored as I stood by his side. It was a humbling experience, but one I had grown used to during the previous year.

The close season is without doubt a wondrous time for footballers. No matter how bad a time a player has had, those six to eight weeks prove miraculous in rejuvenating him for the subsequent season. Tired minds and bodies become fresh and eager for punishment once again. Players return to their clubs full of optimism and enthusiasm, fully believing the new season will be the one for them. Anything is possible at this stage and only when the season commences and bad results follow do any doubts enter their minds.

Most players at that time regarded the close season as a time to do nothing, and very few remained physically active. The time for fitness was during pre-season training, and the summer break was regarded essential for much-needed rest. This attitude has changed over the years, to such an extent that most players continue some form of training during the summer. Many realise that the fitness they have attained during the season can be maintained with a light programme of exercise. If fitness is allowed to deteriorate, pre-season training becomes an agonising ordeal. Bodies seize up and become rigid as muscles become full of lactic acid. Players are then susceptible to tears and strains, so setting fitness back even further. The level of fitness in the modern footballer has improved to such a level that training nowadays is practically a year-round necessity.

I reported back for training believing I could secure a place in the team, even though the club had signed Charlie Nicholas from Celtic for £750,000. John Lukic had also been signed, from Leeds United. I was to link up with John some years later at Elland Road. Chris Whyte was another player at Arsenal with whom I was destined to play again at Leeds. I had purchased a flat in Finchley and was prepared for a determined effort to make my Arsenal career a success. I had continued training during the summer in readiness.

We were taken to a training camp in West Germany to undergo most of our preparation. I trained more fiercely than I had ever done before, still believing places in the team were up for grabs. I was not selected to start our friendly matches, but came on as substitute on several occasions and scored.

It gradually became obvious that there was no place for me, no matter how hard I tried. The manager had already decided upon his team – and I was not in it. Most managers will have a good idea of their starting line-up well before the season begins, but will not divulge this fact, purely for the sake of competition. Any player who is out of the first team must have hopes of breaking into it. Without this motivation, there is no point in his remaining. When it finally dawned on me that there was no place available, I became extremely deflated.

It was around this time that a young member of the first team, who later went on to gain full England caps, purchased his first new car. It was obviously his pride and joy, and he treated it as though it was a newborn baby. I had arranged to meet him in town one day, and was surprised to see him turn up in a cab. I asked him why he had not travelled in his recent purchase, expecting to be told about some kind of repair work or service being done. Instead I received a baffling reply: the car had already travelled too many miles that week, so he was unable to use it until the next.

I was completely dumbfounded and asked for an explanation. It seemed that the salesman at the garage had told him he could travel a maximum of 192 miles a week in his new vehicle. 'So what would happen if during a journey you reached your limit?' I enquired. 'I would pull over and get a cab home,' he replied.

At first I thought he was joking, but I soon realised he was very serious. I tried in vain to make him see reason, by telling him that new cars were only limited by their maximum speed during their running-in period and that mileage was unlimited. He was adamant, and only after a week of ridicule from the other players did he eventually realise his error. The salesman had told him that new cars do an average of ten thousand miles a year – a fact he had taken literally, dividing this figure by fifty-two to get 192 miles per week. Footballers can become worldly at an early age and yet be so very naive at the same time.

The 1983-84 season was four weeks old when Tony Woodcock sustained an injury and I was recalled in his place against Norwich. I scored in a 3–0 victory, much to my delight. I played only two more games before Tony reported fit and reclaimed his place. They were to be my final matches in an Arsenal shirt, a later substitute appearance excepted.

I remained at Highbury for a further three months, and in that time I was able to observe the career of another promising young-ster who had been drawn to London only to be disappointed by it.

Charlie Nicholas had been a scoring sensation in Scotland for Celtic, and had had the choice of the top clubs in England – Manchester United and Liverpool to name but two. He chose Arsenal because of its location. London's bright lights have had a strong attraction for many promising players over the years. He also made his choice on the basis of certain verbal promises which were made to him by the club, regarding financial and playing aspects at Highbury. He was to learn, like many players before him, that promises not written down in a player's contract are rarely kept.

Charlie was very similar to myself – he was young and single and enjoyed a good time, just as most people of that age do. He was also very newsworthy and of extreme interest to the tabloid news-papers. They were determined to create an image of Charlie as a flamboyant, nightclubbing playboy, whether it was true or not. At first he was happy to go along with this, not realising the conse-quences it might have. His agent was also pushing him into high-profile situations and helping to create the picture. Before Charlie realised it, it was too late and the mould had been set. Any subsequent poor performance was blamed on his supposed lifestyle, even though he was doing exactly as he had done during his time in Glasgow.

Charlie arrived at Highbury at a time when some journalists were hailing him as the new George Best. He undoubtedly possessed enormous potential that for many seasons he failed to fulfil. One can only contemplate the thought that if he had moved to Liverpool, his career might have reached the heights many thought possible. At Anfield, players are matured at reserve-team level until they are ready for the first team. They are also controlled by a quiet form of traditional discipline which would have stopped Charlie from participating in the off-the-field publicity stunts which contributed to his flamboyant image.

Not only had Charlie moved to a city that offered many distractions, he had also joined a team that were little more than competent. At Celtic, most of Charlie's effective work was accomplished in the opposition penalty area. At Highbury, after a brief spell as a forward, he was used in a more withdrawn midfield position, thus reducing his effectiveness. Arsenal were also renowned as being a somewhat negative outfit, with all players being required to share defensive duties. Charlie had never been asked to perform these tasks in Scotland.

If Charlie could turn back the clock, I am sure that, like myself, he would do many things differently. The benefit of hindsight would be a great asset to us all, but especially so to young, impressionable footballers moving to London. Nevertheless, Charlie did become a favourite of the North Bank, partly due to his goalscoring exploits against Tottenham. Despite this, his career faded badly and after a lengthy spell out of the team he moved to Aberdeen for a vastly reduced fee.

I endured my Highbury ordeal until the Christmas of 1983. December had been a month of notable dismissals. Richie Barker was sacked by Stoke City in the second week of that month, as the club languished next to the bottom of the First Division. Interestingly for me, two of the club's most influential players, Mickey Thomas and Sammy McIlroy, came off the transfer list following his departure.

More significantly, Terry Neill was dismissed by Arsenal nine days before Christmas, and Don Howe was given temporary charge. I immediately arranged a meeting with Don in an attempt to resurrect my stagnating career. We both agreed it was in my best interests to move to another club. He asked me if there was any-where I would like to go, and I replied that I was sure my old manager, Alan Durban, would be interested.

Alan was now at Sunderland and although the club were in the lower reaches of the First Division, I envisaged a return to the sort of environment I had experienced at Stoke. I contacted Alan, who expressed interest and said he would try and agree a fee with Don Howe. They settled on a figure of £100,000 and a meeting was arranged with Alan at Highbury the following day. On the morn-ing of the meeting I called Alan and insisted my accountant be pre-sent at our meeting. Those were the days when agents and advisers were frowned upon by many managers, Alan included. Neither of us would budge and the move was called off.

Three days later, I backed down, accepted a drop in wages and moved to Sunderland. I was desperate to get away.

My last contact with the Arsenal players had been the occasion of our Christmas party. The annual Yuletide drink is a long-stand-ing tradition at all football clubs. It is one of those times when apprentices and professionals of all ages meet and socialise, the lunchtime party often still in full swing late into the night. Arsenal's party this particular year was held at a luncheon club called School Dinners. Waitresses dress as schoolgirls and cus-tomers take lunch while watching a *risqué* stageshow. These annual get-togethers are always better held in private. The drink flows, and if rival supporters are present, friction can result. On this occasion there were a number of Tottenham fans in the restau-rant who had been consuming large amounts of drink.

A nasty incident occurred, which left Alan Sunderland with a nasty gash to his neck. One of the Spurs fans had broken a piece of mirror off the toilet wall and attacked Alan while he sat at his table. Although the wound merited numerous stitches in a nearby hospital, Alan was fortunate in that the injury could have been much more serious.

Sometimes a few drinks can clear your mind and enable deci-sions to be made. I decided that day that I had to get away at all costs. I contacted Alan Durban the following morning and accepted all his conditions, leaving London with such alacrity that my share of the bill for food and drink was left unpaid – a fact I am constantly reminded of by my Leeds team-mate, John Lukic, who was also present at the lunch.

If there is no worse place than London to have a bad time, then

Sunderland must come a close second. My only reason for moving to this so called sleeping giant was their manager, Alan Durban. I naively thought that his mere presence would guarantee a return to the success I had enjoyed at Stoke. If I had thought long and hard about it I might have questioned such a move, but my desperation to escape from my predicament at Arsenal was such that I gave it little consideration.

Sunderland is not a place to raise the spirits. It is a drab, sombre city with a piercing cold wind off the North Sea that makes it feel many degrees colder than it actually is. This is counterbalanced, however, by the genuine warmth and good nature of the town's inhabitants. It was a pleasant change to be amongst people who had time for each other.

Instead of putting me in hotel accommodation, the club informed me I was to stay in a hostel along with the apprentices and other young professionals. As a cost-cutting exercise this had been club policy for some time, and as all the recent signings had been given the same treatment, I did not object. I was keen to do well at my new club and did not want to create any friction at such an early stage. At least I had the luxury of my own room, even though it was barely large enough for a single bed.

The difference in stature between the club I had left and the one I had joined was very much apparent. Although Arsenal were not doing well on the field, everything off it was geared for success. Things were done properly, no matter what was involved – hotel accommodation, training facilities and general preparation for matches. At Sunderland, everything had the appearance of being second-rate, with cost-cutting economies apparently seeming to be of paramount importance. This even meant that the first team reported to the hostel for pre-match meals.

Roker Park itself looked distinctly shabby and decrepit compared to Highbury. People had talked of Sunderland's vast potential for some time and are still doing so. It became obvious to me soon after my arrival where many of their problems lay. The talk amongst the players and reporters was of a vicious power struggle at boardroom level. For any club to be successful, everybody involved with the running of it must be pulling together in the same direction. With the depressing rumours that this was not the case at Roker Park, their relegation the following season was in many ways inevitable.

I made a bright goalscoring start to my stay at Sunderland scoring four goals in my first eight games. Unfortunately I did not make the same kind of start in my relationship with chairman Tom Cowie, the head of the Cowie Ford dealership empire. I was in between cars and had asked the club to loan me a car for a couple of weeks. Alan Durban agreed to help and managed to obtain a car from one of the chairman's garages. Shortly afterwards I was involved in a crash, resulting in extensive damage to the car, which I returned to the garage for repairs, safe in the knowledge that I was covered by their insurance.

Two days later I was summoned to the chairman's office. He was extremely unhappy about the damage to his car and wanted me to pay for all the repairs. I thought it was only fair the costs should be borne by the insurance company. Neither of us would budge and I was shown the door with the words, 'Don't expect any help from me in the future!' It was the first and only conversation I would ever have with him.

I had been with the club for only nine games when Alan Durban was dismissed. Eight matches without a win had been enough to end Alan's reign. It came as a great shock to me after only two months at the club. He had been the only reason for my presence, and now he was gone I began to doubt the wisdom of the move. I felt desperately sorry for Alan and somehow responsible for his demise. He was a good manager and not the first – nor the last – to suffer such a fate at Sunderland.

My worst fears were confirmed when Len Ashurst was appointed as the new manager. A Liverpudlian, his greatest successes in management had come with Newport County and Gillingham, although Sheffield Wednesday supporters remember him as the man who took his players on survival courses on desolate moorland.

His first meeting with the Sunderland players was so contrived it was almost farcical. It is the only time I have known a new manager to bring the chairman with him to meet the players. It was not so much a meeting as a lecture that was obviously meant to impress the attendant Tom Cowie. It struck me as the most insincere speech I had ever heard. We were told of the hardship we should expect in return for playing for 'this great club'. We were even told we would have to 'eat rocks'. The chairman might have been impressed, but the players were definitely not.

Ashurst had several ideas I thought odd both in training and for matches. Most clubs wind down training on a Thursday and Friday before a match. We were made to lap the pitch on several occasions on Thursday, training normally only carried out at the beginning of the week.

My situation came to a head as we prepared for an away match at Stoke. We were made to warm up in the dressing room by jogging on the spot and then intermittently sprinting flat out while emitting a piercing scream. We had done this since Ashurst's arrival and it had become a standing joke. Unknown to him, the players had begun to utter more and more bloodcurdling screams in an attempt to ridicule the procedure. He obviously took the increased noise as a sign of extra commitment. Unfortunately I could hold my mirth no longer and started to giggle. His eyes met mine and his look said it all – no one would take the mickey out of him.

I was substituted that game and dropped for the following one. It is never pleasant to be omitted, but this time I had expected it. It was obvious that our time together would be limited, and I would have to leave. Len Ashurst was a man I could not work for. There were eight games left of the season, and I did not expect to play for Sunderland again. I began to train and play with renewed vigour in an attempt to get a move as soon as possible.

The final match of the season approached. It was away at Leicester, and Sunderland needed to win to be assured of First Division status. I was taken aside by the manager the day before the game and told that he was going to play me and that several clubs were watching me. It was a great piece of psychology – I played my finest match in a Sunderland shirt and scored in a 2–0 victory.

After the match we were taken to a hotel by the directors for a champagne celebration, which speaks volumes for Sunderland's ambitions and priorities. It was the flattest party I have ever been to. I confronted the manager and demanded to know which clubs had been present at the game. He refused to tell me, which frustrated me further. I told him in no uncertain terms that I wanted to leave the club, and he turned and walked away.

Before he left, Alan Durban had arranged an end-of-season holiday to Magaluf. That seemed to be all I had to look forward to now.

· 5 ·

Howard's way to happier days

The English season demands the greatest feats of endurance in world football. It takes enormous powers of self-motivation and concentration to perform at a consistently high standard for its duration, something that is particularly difficult for younger players to achieve. These attributes are acquired over a period of years by those who become successful and go on to have distinguished careers in the game. Those who do not acquire them are bound to fall by the wayside.

Success and failure bring pressures to bear in their own particular ways. The successful have set themselves standards which, at the very least, need to be equalled year after year. The failures know, if they possess the right attitude, that they must improve, or end up on the football scrapheap. I fell very much into the latter category as I finished the season with Sunderland. My previous two years could definitely not be described as being triumphant – in fact for most of the period I was an abject failure. I knew I had reached a crucial point in my career where one thing was obvious: I had to break the cycle of failure. I had reached rock bottom at Arsenal and had merely bobbled along it at Sunderland. I could not go any lower, and I decided there was only one route for me now. My saving grace was that I still retained a semblance of self-belief, even after all I had been through.

As I made my way to Mallorca with Sunderland I decided there was little I could do during the next frivolous week in terms of career advancement. How wrong I was.

The end-of-season break is something that the majority of clubs arrange for their players, and in some cases the players provide for themselves. It is generally anticipated with great relish, especially amongst the young and single. It marks the end of the season and the beginning of six to eight weeks of relaxation away from football. However good or bad or indifferent the season has been, it is an excuse for teams to celebrate or forget the previous ten months of hard slog.

For some the trip becomes a farewell to those they have worked with so closely. It seemed certain this would be the case for me. I knew there was no possibility of forming a working relationship with Len Ashurst, and that one of us would have to go. Ashurst had only recently been appointed and was sure of another season at the helm. I could not afford to wait: another year like the previous two would have done irreparable damage to my career.

Even during my short time at the club, I had felt more a part of the team than I ever had at Arsenal. Maybe it was a reflection of the area, but the players and staff were noticeably warmer. The squad included Barry Venison (later to play for Liverpool), Paul Bracewell (my ex-team-mate at Stoke), Mark Proctor (a future team-mate at Sheffield Wednesday), and Bryan 'Pop' Robson (the veteran goalscorer) to name a few. During teams trips, players usually split up into two or three groups. My room partner was Mark Proctor, and we found ourselves teaming up with goalkeeper Chris Turner (later to play for Manchester United and Sheffield Wednesday) and another seasoned striker, Gary Rowell.

Halfway through the week, we found ourselves in a smart restaurant on the outskirts of Palma Nova. We had had a good meal, and were enjoying a few *digestifs*, when we were joined by Sheffield Wednesday's assistant manager, Peter Eustace, and director Cliff Woodward. Peter had recently been the coach at Sunderland under Alan Durban and although we had never met, he knew the rest of the players at the table very well.

The drinks flowed along with the conversation. Most of the team were unhappy at that time, Chris included. He had recently mentioned his desire to play once again for Wednesday and was dropping blatant hints to Peter at every opportunity. Peter pointed out that the goalkeeping position was covered, but that they were searching for a centre forward. With my intake of booze to spur me on, I was talking freely, and passionately expressed my desire to resurrect my career with another club. Peter was obviously impressed and asked if I would like to play for Wednesday: I would. Then came the bombshell – would I take a cut in wages? Of course I would. He was now extremely interested and left the table with my phone number, saying he would be in touch. It had come completely out of the blue, but I sensed a real possibility that my career might take a step in the right direction.

Wednesday had just been promoted to the First Division after a lengthy period of exile. It was a fresh start for them, and it could mean the same for me if Peter was as interested as he seemed. That summer I thought of nothing else and waited patiently for a call.

It came three weeks before the date on which pre-season training traditionally began. Wednesday, however, were reporting for training before anybody else. The call was from manager Howard Wilkinson, who asked if I had meant what I said in Mallorca. If so, could I ring Len Ashurst and then phone him back. My call to Ashurst was short and to the point. He had agreed a fee with Sheffield but would be happy if I stayed. I did not hesitate. I made it clear I intended to move and we said goodbye.

My next call was to Howard Wilkinson to arrange a meeting place for contractual talks the following day. We met and, true to my word, I took my second successive drop in wages. This time the move felt right. I was impressed by the manager and his desire to do well. I was impressed by the stadium, and the enormous potential the club seemed to have. Most of all it was a chance to join a club whose fortunes had been similar to my own – we had both experienced hard times, but now there was a chance to re-establish ourselves among the elite.

I signed for the same fee that Sunderland had paid Arsenal – £100,000. The drop in wages was not pleasant, but at that time, money was a secondary consideration. My career and personal happiness were uppermost in my mind.

Little did I know then that my association with Howard Wilkinson would be long and successful, encompassing two different clubs. My initial impressions of him were of a dour, determined Yorkshireman with a mission in life. He intended to go to the top in management, but he was going to do it his own way, which turned out to be completely different from any other in my experience. His teams report back for training earlier than anyone else – although over the years many more have brought their dates forward – and they are required to complete six weeks of pre-season training, with a four-or five-day break given after four of those weeks have been negotiated.

A lot of Howard's earlier beliefs have been rethought and changed or adapted over the years. One of his early policies at Wednesday was the introduction of his infamous cross-country runs. These started in pre-season training and were continued throughout the season on a Monday or Tuesday whenever there was no midweek game. The length and regularity of these runs soon became legendary throughout the world of football, but their severity eventually became a barrier to the club's attempts to sign new players. I met several people, and heard of others on the grapevine, who were put off joining Wednesday by tales of these runs.

The runs took place in hilly areas beyond Sheffield, in Yorkshire countryside that was beautiful in summer but very bleak in winter. All runs lasted at least forty-five minutes, but could extend to ninety or more. The longest run I undertook was thirteen miles, the length of a half-marathon. Most of the smaller players adapted well to this strenuous training, but some of the larger ones suffered badly and were left trailing by huge distances. Many players would often lose their way, notably centre forward Tony Cunningham and goalkeeper Iain Hesford. They had even been know to hitch lifts on a passing farmer's tractor.

During the winter, the runs became tests of endurance. Snow and sub-zero temperatures were commonplace, with frostbitten hands and feet to match. We would often run through twelve inches of snow and slide down hazardous slopes. Inevitably, this was done with more than a little cursing and swearing. The players' annoyance with the manager and their combined efforts to complete the course brought them closer together as a team – something I am sure the manager knew only too well. He was a great admirer of army techniques and their psychology value in forming a close-knit unit.

My first pre-season at Wednesday was a real shock to the system. I woke up some mornings barely able to walk to the bathroom, such was the stiffness in my muscles. Like any new recruit, I gradually acclimatised and soon grew accustomed to the new regime. We had barely started training when we began rehearsing set-piece plays – corners, throw-ins and free kicks. Many clubs did not rehearse these at all, and those that did left it until the day before a match. We spent many arduous hours over set-pieces, both before and during the season. Friday mornings during the season became notorious for these lengthy sessions, which would often last for over two hours. Set-pieces were rehearsed as though we were in a match situation, and any lack of commitment was frowned upon.

Preparation was, and still is, an obsession with Howard, although the severity of many of his methods has been reduced over the years. He has not rigidly stuck to his original theories and beliefs, but has adapted and in some cases changed them completely.

In those early days at Wednesday, I got the impression that Howard thought he could transform a squad of competent players into a team capable of competing with the best. He also believed he could transform the fortunes of problem players or those who had fallen on hard times (I was in the latter category).

His squad was a mixture of lower-division signings, local players and those just mentioned. The resources to buy top players were not made available to him. Instead, armed with his beliefs, he decided to implement a long-ball game. This type of game enables a manager working within a tight budget to produce a team that is not attractive to watch, but is very effective. It relies not on keeping possession of the ball, but on delivering it into the opponent's final third of the pitch and then pressurising this area. The ball is immediately delivered into the penalty area, and then pressurised again. It is akin to a rugby union team that favours a kicking game, and demands a high level of fitness from the players concerned, especially the midfielders, who are completely missed out as the ball progresses into the opponent's half. They are virtually required to run between the two penalty areas for the entire ninety minutes.

The very nature of this type of game necessitates a high turnover of players. It is not only physically demanding, it also requires a high level of motivation among those taking part. After all, football is all about possession of the ball, and the long-ball game is based on chasing it rather than its retention. Managers who espouse this type of football are widely criticised and scorned, but it is interesting to put yourself in the manager's shoes. What would any young manager do when faced with the dilemma of playing nice football, losing and getting the sack, or playing the long-ball game, winning and retaining his job? For some who rely on football for a living there is no choice, and that is why this type of football has gained popularity among managers, especially in the lower divisions, where clubs with financial problems are commonplace. The game's best managers tend to be those who are at the wealthiest clubs.

Whatever the style of football there is always a need for honesty in a player. Honesty is a vital factor in any successful team. A dishonest player will create ill-feeling and discontent among the others in the dressing room, and a good atmosphere is vital. That is one requirement Howard constantly demands from a player, and if it is not forthcoming, the association between the two is always short-lived.

The atmosphere at Hillsborough was ideal. There was a terrific spirit throughout the squad, even among those who were not in the first team. It was exactly what I needed after the previous two years – at last I felt at home.

The 1984–85 season started well, with a 3–1 home victory against Nottingham Forest. That win set us up for a successful first season back in the First Division, with notable victories at Liverpool and Manchester United. We finished a creditable eighth in the League, reached the quarter-finals of the League Cup, and I personally finished with a goal tally of twenty. It was my best-ever total for a season, and exactly the kick-start my flagging career needed.

With me at Hillsborough were players like Martin Hodge, the goalkeeper I had played with at Plymouth. Others included John Pearson, Mel Sterland and Imre Varadi, who were all to link up with me at Leeds United a few years later.

The club possessed some great characters, like goalkeeper Iain Hesford, who was a great mimic. His speciality was the backward supporter asking for an autograph. Every club seems to possess one and Iain's interpretation was wickedly accurate. He also had a liking for a pint, something that did not help his weight problem. The manager eventually banned Iain from frequenting pubs, in an attempt to decrease his bulk. Unfortunately for Iain, just as he was entering his local one evening, coach Peter Eustace happened to be driving by. The following morning he was hauled into the office by the manager and told that a heavy fine was imminent unless he could produce an explanation. Iain's response was brilliant. The previous evening, he said, his pet dog had run away and he had gone to look for it. His search had taken him past the pub in question, and the reason he had been seen entering was that he had gone to ask the landlord if there had been any sighting of his beloved hound. After an excuse like that, the manager had to let him off, even though he knew it to be pure fabrication.

Another character was the veteran centre half Mick Lyons, who had enjoyed a distinguished career at his beloved Everton. Even though he was now a Wednesday player, 'Lyonsy' became very depressed whenever his ex-team suffered defeat. A more passionate and committed player I have yet to meet. He was the team captain and led purely by example. His pre-match warm-up consisted of his heading a ball tossed over the head of a standing colleague. On one occasion, he was so highly motivated that he followed through, causing a violent clash of heads. Several stitches were needed to close a gaping wound in Lyonsy's forehead, and all that was before the kick off!

This commitment even extended to our Christmas party. Lyonsy had decreed that everybody should turn up in fancy dress. Unknown to him we decided to set him up and come in normal attire. He turned up authentically dressed as a caveman, almost naked except for a sheepskin wrap-around and a pair of sandals. He had also managed to obtain a three-foot-long animal thigh-bone, which still had pieces of bloodied flesh dangling from it. Even though he had been set up, he carried this revolting bone throughout the subsequent pub crawl around Sheffield's city centre. At the end of the evening, he was a disgusting sight, his hands and legs almost entirely covered in congealed blood.

During the 1984-85 season, I had missed only three matches, all through injury. On each occasion, my place had been taken by John Pearson, a centre forward of similar stature to myself. John, although a good player, was a genuinely nice person and not the slightest bit aggressive, something that has stopped him scoring more goals during his career. The manager was well aware of this and had tried everything he could think of to instil some aggression.

We were due to play Coventry at Hillsborough, a game I was unable to participate in through injury. John was my replacement and was standing around in his jockstrap prior to the match in a very relaxed state. The manager was at the end of his tether, seeing John so laid-back before a big game, and he marched up to him and asked him if he was going to be in an aggressive mood in time for the match. John's reply was to giggle an unconvincing 'yes'. Through pure frustration, the manager delivered two sharp blows to his face, one to either cheek. The dressing room suddenly hushed in anticipation of the reaction to these considerable blows. Even Howard braced himself, quite hoping for some kind of response. He got one. John's face lit up with a broad smile from ear to ear. It seemed nothing could make him lose his temper. In spite of everything, he went on to score the only goal of the game.

At the end of the season, the club went to Thailand to play an exhibition game against Graham Taylor's Watford. The idea was to play the match in Bangkok and then travel to Pattaya for several days' holiday.

Up until the match, our players behaved sensibly, but then treated the remaining time as a chance to relax and have a bit of fun. This was in stark contrast to the Watford squad who seemed unable to participate in anything light-hearted. We were hard pressed to find any of them with a smile on their faces, except Nigel Callaghan, who ended up going out with the Wednesday players instead of his own. Graham Taylor had a reputation for being a strict disciplinarian and it seemed his players were not allowed to enjoy themselves, even though the season was over.

The build-up to the 1985-86 season saw the acquisition of the usual mixture of lower-division players and those who were down on their luck. The new players who, like myself, had shown great promise and then slumped were Mark Chamberlain, Garry Thompson and Simon Stainrod, who had signed at the end of the previous season. Such players appealed to the manager, who was convinced he could transform their fortunes. Lower-division signings included Glynn Snodin from Doncaster Rovers and Carl Shutt from non-League Spalding Town. Paul Hart was another new recruit. He had previously been at Nottingham Forest and before that Leeds, two clubs I was later to play for.

Harty and I hit it off instantly, and became room partners on away trips. He had been heavily influenced by his time with Brian Clough and believed in the work-hard-and-play-hard philosophy. We were like two mischievous schoolboys together, with neither of us needing much encouragement, although any forthcoming match was always treated with respect.

Our pre-season build-up involved a trip to Finland. After a week of playing matches, training very hard and generally doing a lot of travelling, we were given a much-needed day off which signalled a chance for the lads to have a few beers. The manager had other ideas and arranged a boat trip on a nearby lake. Attendance was compulsory and a disappointed group of players boarded a large cruiser vessel. It was to be a two-hour trip and after ten minutes we realised it was going to be a test of endurance. The manager and Peter Eustace were in their element on deck, pointing out various types of trees and birds.

In our boredom, Paul Hart and myself wandered below deck to

find a seat. To our surprise we entered a comfortable lounge area equipped with a fully stocked bar, waitress and stereo system. We quickly went back on deck and whispered the news to a carefully selected few. Minutes later, a party was in full swing. The manager and coach stayed out on deck the whole time, completely unaware of the activities below. When the boat docked, those below deck staggered off having enjoyed a marvellous cruise.

Dressing-room banter is more often than not centred around the mickey-taking or winding up of those who leave themselves open to it. This generally involves those new to the professional game, those new to the club or those who will always leave themselves wide open, no matter how long they are in the game. Everybody at some stage goes through this initiation process until they too are sharp enough to reverse the roles.

Carl Shutt was an obvious candidate for a wind-up. He was fresh from non-League football and was showing such a degree of naivety that it begged to be tested. It soon came when injuries demanded he should make his First Division debut after only two months at the club. Mick Lyons, always the practical joker, came up with the tried and tested formula of impersonating a newspaper reporter. He even involved the manager, who informed Carl at a team meeting that he would be receiving a call from a journalist later that evening. We were quick to offer advice, telling him he was big news now and that he must demand at least £250 for his story. Carl had already acquired a reputation for being somewhat careful with his money, and this advice was music to his ears.

That evening, it was decided I should make the call, as Lyonsy's strong Liverpudlian accent would have given the game away. Although Carl was not familiar with any journalists, I pretended to be David Walker from the *Daily Mail*. I established that I had been given permission by the manager to speak to him, and asked him if he was willing to answer a few questions. He said he would, but only if he was paid. I smiled and asked him how much he would want. I almost broke into laughter when he nervously demanded £350, a hundred more than we had told him to ask for.

I said that it was a lot of money, but that I could get it for him if he consented to have his picture taken as well. He agreed and I began the interview. In this situation it is standard practice to ask the player being wound up what he thinks of the players competing for his position. In many cases I have known a victim to be severely critical of his colleagues in off-the-record comments. Carl was extremely diplomatic, even when questioned about myself and whether he thought he should be playing ahead of me.

At the end of the call I arranged a time for a photographer to meet him before training. I told him that as he had been a mechanic before turning professional, the paper would want a picture of him in his work overalls, holding some of his tools. He agreed. For £350 I think he would have gone along with almost anything.

The following morning we arranged for the club photographer, Steve Ellis, to turn up shortly before training. Everyone had been notified and we all waited expectantly. Carl showed up, as requested, with neatly pressed overalls and a box of tools. He donned the overalls and was persuaded to leap in the air holding a wrench in one hand and a hammer in the other. He repeated this exercise several times until the hysterical laughter from the whole squad brought the sickening realisation – he had been set up.

This embarrassing experience was soon brushed aside, however, as we formed a successful attacking partnership that resulted in our both scoring against Coventry in a 2–2 draw.

The season had been something of a surprise to me. After my successful first year, I found myself competing with Simon Stainrod and Garry Thompson for two striking positions. The start of the campaign had seen us all lose our places in the team as the manager experimented with his best line-up. After the previous season, I realised I could not return to the obscurity of reserve-team football once again, and I met the challenge with confident determination. I established my place alongside Garry Thompson, which led to Simon Stainrod's departure to Aston Villa.

Two big men as attacking partners is not the ideal pairing. Both players tend to take the same positions, which inevitably leads to one of the pair playing in an unfamiliar role in order to accommodate the other. However, my prolonged taste of failure had given me a tremendous strength as I rebuilt my career. I had experienced success again, and the one thing which would guarantee its continuation was my ability to score goals. With this fear of failure driving me on, I became the dominant partner and Garry was left to improvise. This undoubtedly affected Garry's game as the first half of the season brought him a total of two goals to my twelve. Garry had cost almost half a million pounds, and the manager's judgement was being questioned. His response was to omit me from the team after a run of twelve goals in twenty-four games.

After missing three matches, I returned only for illness to strike. I had been experiencing severe stomach pains late at night for a few weeks. It was diagnosed as acute indigestion, but my consumption of vast quantities of strong antacid suspension did nothing to alleviate my problem. On the morning of our evening game against Leicester, I had been unable to take part in set-piece rehearsals due to abdominal pains, my first attack during the day. I played the match in agony and trundled wearily off at the end. I hardly had the strength to change, but somehow managed to make my way home.

The following morning I awoke to find my skin had a yellow tinge to it and my urine was a dark-brown colour. Something was seriously wrong. Physiotherapist Alan Smith sent me straight to a specialist who diagnosed me as being jaundiced. Blood samples were taken and I was found to be suffering from the non-specific A strain of hepatitis which I had probably contracted from infected food. I was ordered to take complete rest for two months and to abstain from alcohol for one year, as well as eating a fat-free diet. The timing could not have been worse – we were due to play Everton in the semi-final of the FA Cup in three weeks' time.

During my first week of recuperation I found it tiring merely to walk. This soon passed as I quickly started to regain my strength. I had never ruled myself out of the semi-final, even though the specialist definitely had. Halfway through the third week, I contacted the manager and told him I was fit enough to resume training. I reported directly to the team's training base at Lilleshall, where preparations were being made for the big game. After two training sessions I was told, to my surprise, that I would be playing.

We travelled to a hotel in Birmingham in readiness for the tie at Villa Park. On the morning of the game, a religious convention was being held inside the hotel. We were informed that we were to be blessed by some of the clergy prior to our departure. As we queued for our blessing, goalkeeper Martin Hodge, our captain, hardly inspired confidence when he remarked, 'It will take more than this for us to win today'.

He was right: we were beaten 2–1 and I was substituted at 1–1 when fatigue had set in. It was my second semi-final defeat at Villa Park, the first one having been with Arsenal in 1983 when I came on as substitute against Manchester United.

I played three more League games before I was forced to sit out the remainder of the season. It had been a strange season for me.

The team had finished fifth, and although top scorer, I had missed many matches due to illness and competition for places. It seemed I had survived both when Garry Thompson was sold to Aston Villa shortly after the season had finished. Even though we had at times been fierce rivals, we became close friends and in that respect I was sad to see him leave.

Another player no longer at the club was Mick Lyons, who was transferred to Grimsby as player-manager early in the season. He was another friend whose presence in the dressing room was sadly missed. There is little room for sentiment in football, a game where the constant movement of players and managers is inevitable.

Midfielder Andy Blair was yet another to be shown the proverbial door. The manager's frustration with the midfielder he had played since Wednesday's return to the First Division was obviously reaching crisis point. It did so during an FA Cup tie at Derby, when Andy's nonchalant back pass to an opposing player resulted in a goal against us. He was immediately substituted, never to kick a ball for the club again.

Football is also a game that is constantly producing quirks of fate – Gary Megson had been signed by Howard Wilkinson for the second time, so bringing us together once again after our brief spell at Plymouth.

I had signed a two-year contract on my arrival from Sunderland and it was now nearing its end. I was actually in a position that I had not been in since my early days at Stoke – I wanted to stay where I was.

Sheffield is a big city, but in many respects is a conglomeration of villages, with a village atmosphere to match. The city has plenty to offer, both in terms of nightlife and amenities, as well as having inhabitants that are warm and friendly with a strong passion for their football. Hillsborough was a magnificent place to play every other week, and it still remains one of my favourite stadiums. The famous 'Kop' was covered and extended during my time there, making the atmosphere inside the ground a joy to experience.

The club also attracted its fair share of glamour. Members of the pop band the Human League were regular visitors to matches, as well as Martyn Ware, leader of the group Heaven 17. Martyn was also an ex-member of the Human League and went on to produce albums for people like Terence Trent D'Arby and Tina Turner. He was an avid fan who travelled to most games, home and away, from his London base. It seemed the least I could do was to supply him with tickets and the occasional room for the night. Other famous 'Wednesdayites' included Labour MPs Joe Ashton, who later joined the board of directors, and Roy Hattersley. Roy even joined us on one occasion for our pre-match meal.

The club held a lot of appeal for me and it seemed that I appealed to its manager. Initially, I may have been a short-term signing until somebody else could be brought in. These players were purchased, but in each case I managed to withstand the competition to such an extent that their time at the club was short-lived. I had become a fighter, with a desperate desire not to return to the dark days of Arsenal. I had also discovered a level of commitment, albeit naive, that saw me suffer numerous injuries, mainly facial and head wounds that needed a total of over a hundred stitches in my two years at Hillsborough. My ability to bounce quickly back from these injuries, and also my fight against hepatitis, I am sure convinced Howard that I was the right man for the job. With this in mind, we agreed upon a much-improved two-year contract.

The build-up to the 1986-87 season saw a distinct change in the team's style of play. For the previous two years, we had become infamous for our long-ball game, in much the same way as Wimbledon and Crystal Palace have now. We had received a great deal of criticism because of it, mainly from the football purists. The manager was now making a determined attempt to play a more cultured game. The midfield was no longer bypassed, but involved directly in the team's build-up play. For the previous two years, the midfield players had spent the entire game basically running from penalty box to penalty box, a frustrating way for them to play. This new style was proving to be considerably more enjoyable.

It was at this stage that the club's lack of ambition became evident. To play a cultured game requires the team to possess players of great ability. I have no doubt that an influx of quality at this time would have enabled the team to compete with the best. Instead, the manager's hands were tied and he was only able to make his usual quota of minor signings. The board, led by chairman Bert McGee, seemed to us to show an alarming lack of foresight and seemed to be content with just First Division status. It is ironic that it took the subsequent departure of Howard to Leeds to revolutionise their way of thinking.

With this attitude prevalent, the team's ability to improve was always going to be restricted, something the players were well aware of. If ambition is missing at boardroom level, it is only a matter of time before it creeps into the minds of players.

One of the season's minor signings was that of David Hirst from Barnsley for £200,000. He was then a raw youngster with pace and a blistering shot. He had a good attitude, but was sometimes very naive, a trait that earned him the nickname 'Pikey' after the character in the television comedy *Dad's Army*. Many of his comments were met with the retort, 'Stupid boy', in the fashion of Captain Mainwaring.

His first pre-match meal with the first team proved to be hilarious. A giant plate of bacon sandwiches arrived in front of him, two and a half hours before he was due to play. This had apparently been his pre-match meal at Barnsley. The subsequent ridiculing he received from the rest of the team ensured it was not going to be so at Wednesday.

On a tour to Canada, his description of the Niagara Falls is one I shall not forget. We had been on a tour underneath them and were now observing them from a nearby restaurant, when Hirsty came out with his considered judgement of one of the most amazing sights in the world. 'All they are is just great heaps of watter,' he uttered in his broad Yorkshire accent.

It has been nice to see him mature and develop into the quality player he is today. He always kept that good attitude and you somehow just knew he would make it. Wednesday's initial outlay has proved to be a sound investment, and indeed his valuation has since increased many times over.

Brian Marwood, who later became chairman of the PFA – the players' union – was another who had an interesting nickname. 'Buns' was so called because of his penchant for a snack and the ample shape of his posterior. He was also renowned for obtaining Boss clothing labels from a retailer friend and getting his wife, Lesley, to sew them on his ordinary pieces of clothing. Many of his C & A jackets were magically transformed in this way. Brian became a great pal of mine and it is nice to see his burning desire to help his fellow professionals put to such good use. Brian was a great crosser of the ball and provided me with the supply for many of my goals at Hillsborough.

Gary 'Suitcase' Megson was another in my circle of close friends. The name 'Suitcase' was derived from the fact that he was never at one club for very long – for a midfield player he certainly did move more than most.

The club was filled with an interesting mixture of characters who all combined to create a positive dressing-room atmosphere. Mark Chamberlain, who at one time was being compared favourably to John Barnes, never quite managed to fulfil the exciting potential he displayed at Stoke City. He undoubtedly possessed the ability needed, but for some reason he never blossomed as he should have done. Mark was one of the most laid-back characters I have shared a dressing room with, a fact that was a constant irritation to the manager, who tried everything he knew to spark some life into him.

Mel 'Zico' Sterland, who was another to provide me with some great service in and around the penalty area, earned his name from the Hillsborough faithful for two reasons. One was because of the tremendous shot he possessed and unleashed at vital moments, akin to the legendary Zico of Brazil. The other was a tongue-in-cheek comparison between the nature of the two men. Mel has always enjoyed his food and his stockily built frame provided a vivid contrast to the lithe form of the original Zico.

That season was proving to be an indifferent one for the team as we languished in the lower half of the First Division table. Things took a further turn for the worse when my room partner, Paul Hart, was sold to Birmingham in a hastily arranged deal. 'Fossil' or 'Horlicks', as he was affectionately known, was another character who was to be sorely missed. He was known as 'Fossil' because of his lived-in looks and 'Horlicks' because most of his conversation had the same effect on people as a bedtime drink. Paul did not want to leave, but the fact that the manager had put the deal to him at all was a dent to his pride, and so he moved on. Tragedy struck immediately, when on his debut for Birmingham he suffered a compound fracture to his leg. It was an injury that effectively meant the end of his professional playing career and led him down the rocky road into coaching and management, with all the pitfalls that entails.

Shortly after Paul Hart's terrible injury, cruel misfortune struck again, and this time it happened to a player at the opposite end of the age scale. Paul was approaching his mid-thirties, whereas Ian Knight, a centre half of tremendous potential, was just beginning his first-team career. During an FA Cup replay against Chester City at Hillsborough, an incident occurred that left Ian with the worst injury I have ever witnessed on a football field. He went for a ball that was sixty–forty in his favour against Chester striker Gary Bennett, who had been unfortunately nicknamed 'Psycho' by his supporters. From where I was standing Bennett's subsequent attempt to win the ball from Ian seemed to me to be the most diabolically reckless tackle. It was so high and late it left Ian with a double compound fracture of his leg. Such was the severity of the injury that his fibula had been forced through his calf muscle and out of his sock. The sight of this bone protruding out of his leg turned even the strongest stomach.

Although Ian remarkably made a full recovery, the injury undoubtedly left its mark and made people wonder what he might have achieved. Players have a duty to play hard, but that has to be within the laws of the game. Only Gary Bennett will know whether his actions were premeditated or not, and only he will know why it took a year and a half to make contact with Ian, via a Christmas card.

My colleagues' misfortunes were tempered by happier times for me personally. At around the same time, I met my future wife, Leslie, through a mutual friend in London. Hitherto I had been a free spirit without anybody to answer to. I was now entering a period of stability and undergoing many changes in my lifestyle. These proved to be even greater with the arrival of our children.

Stability can be vital to a footballer's career, but only if he is ready for it. There is a tendency for many footballers to marry at an early age. This occurs for two main reasons. Firstly, they have lots of spare time on their hands because training usually finishes each day at lunchtime, and secondly because footballers are used to being looked after by their parents and club, and many are ill-equipped for life on their own. I have known many who have married early only to regret their actions later and wonder what they are missing out on. Although this happens in most walks of life, in football the opportunities to stray are very much greater.

Ironically, Leslie's arrival on the scene heralded a disastrous run of ten games without a win, which included seven defeats. Supporters in their superstitious way began to regard her as something of a Jonah, and let her know it in no uncertain terms whenever she attended a match.

Two victories were then followed by four more defeats which left us perilously close to the relegation zone. A late rally of three wins and two draws in our final six matches saw us avoid relegation and finish thirteenth in the table. Although I had ended the campaign with twenty-two goals and the team had reached the quarter-finals of the FA Cup, it was in many ways a disappointing season.

Lack of ambition, originating at boardroom level, soon spread throughout the club like a malignant cancer. Players like myself, Brian Marwood, Nigel Worthington and Mel Sterland had once been grateful for the chance to play for a club like Wednesday. We had established our First Division status only to find the club little by little losing hold of theirs.

The signs were there to see before and during my final season at Hillsborough. The start of the 1987-88 season found the manager making the usual mixture of signings – those from the lower divisions, or those with very low fees. You could sense that players like myself were now playing with a view to getting transferred to a more ambitious club. It was quite obvious to all concerned that the club were happy just to survive in the top flight and that any honours in the game would have to be won elsewhere. It seemed nonsensical for a club with such enormous potential to be run in such a short-sighted way.

The season was, predictably, full of inconsistency. I was, amazingly, paired with Colin West with whom I had had an unsuccessful playing liaison at Sunderland, and another recent signing was Mark Proctor, who had also been with me at Sunderland.

It was an unremarkable season, other than an epic FA Cup duel with our bogey team, Everton. The third-round tie went to three replays before Everton came out 5–0 winners. Including a League game, we played them five times in twenty-six days. Most sides have a jinx team, and Everton were ours. If it is common knowledge, this fact can and does play a major psychological part in determining the result of such encounters. The habitual losers often walk on to the pitch with a definite inferiority complex, and similarly the habitual winners have an air of superiority about them. Footballers are a superstitious breed and there is no doubt that many are affected by these quirks of fate.

We may not have had the greatest team in the Football League, but we probably had the brightest. Tony Galvin, the ex-Spurs winger, had a degree in Russian Studies and Lawrie Madden, our veteran centre half, had acquired an Open University degree while at Wednesday.

Football has always been regarded as a working-class game, played by players from working-class backgrounds. This and the apprentice system, whereby youngsters are signed on at the age of sixteen, has meant that the majority of footballers have not been highly educated. This compares strikingly with rugby union, which in England has traditionally been played by those from public schools who have therefore tended to go on to higher education. There are exceptions to the rule and Tony and Lawrie were just two. Footballers are generally categorised as not being too bright and far from eloquent. In years gone by television and radio interviews have done much to enhance this reputation. Players unused to giving interviews tend to talk wholly in football clichés – 'sick as a parrot' and 'over the moon' are just two of the more obvious ones. Footballers still do not receive any education in the techniques of interviews or public speaking. It is little wonder that so many uneducated players sound just that.

As the season drew to a close the rumblings of discontent grew and grew. It seemed to me that even the manager had become disillusioned with life at Wednesday. He did not seem as motivated as he once had been, something that was hardly surprising. Howard was an ambitious manager, who realised he could go no further with the resources at his disposal.

Brian Marwood was the first to leave when he moved to Arsenal for £600,000 shortly before the transfer deadline. This deadline always falls around the middle of March and is a time when players with itchy feet wait for a summons to the manager's office. For the first time in four years, I found myself in just this position. Brian's departure only made me more certain of my desire to move to a more ambitious club, both for career and financial reasons.

A transfer did not materialise, but my contract was due to expire at the end of the season and then I was free to move. I started to contact various agents and expressed a desire to move abroad if the money was right.

I received a boost to my confidence one evening when I took a call from Nottingham Forest's Alan Hill. He enquired whether, if I used my right to freedom of contract, I would want to play for Brian Clough. I needed no time to consider my reply – of course I would. Alan said he would be in touch and said goodbye. I replaced the receiver, excited at the thought of the great man's interest in me.

I was even more excited a few weeks later when I received a call from Uli Hoeness, now the manager of Bayern Munich. I was informed of the club's interest and asked if I could meet them in London after our penultimate game of the season at Wimbledon. He was going to watch me play and then meet me in the Grill Room at the Savoy Hotel.

The match was drawn 1–1, but I managed to score and gave a good account of myself. Afterwards I met Hoeness and an assistant to discuss the possibility of a move. I was asked if I would go on trial at the end of the season. Despite my refusal Hoeness still wanted to sign me. He had seen enough during the game, but would have to get the agreement of the coach, whose job it was to pick the team. On the Continent coaches deal wholly with the playing side, and the managers are responsible solely for finances. The coach would travel to our final game of the season and make his judgement.

Our final match was at home to Liverpool who had run away with the League championship by some considerable margin. I desperately wanted to move abroad, and the chance of playing for one of the greatest European clubs thrilled me. I was ready to give the performance of a lifetime and felt extremely confident as I walked on to the field for what I was sure was my final appearance in Wednesday colours.

Liverpool then proceeded to give one of their finest ever performances, playing football that should only be possible in dreams. We were humiliated 5–1 – a scoreline that actually flattered us. I and the rest of my colleagues barely received a kick.

As I trundled despondently off the pitch, I knew my move to Bayern had been cruelly crushed. It came as no surprise to me when all contact with the Germans ceased.

·6·

Lost in France –
the Maxwell saga

If I had answered the phone during the summer of 1988 to find an
agent asking me to join Crewe Alexandra, I would probably have
thought it was a practical joke by my Sheffield Wednesday partners in crime. When the call came from Niort, the French equivalent of Crewe in terms of both town and team, I jumped at the
chance.

It was a time of great upheaval in my life – much of it self-
inflicted – which began with my turning down an offer from Elton
John to join Watford and ended after a tug-of-war between those
footballing heavyweights Robert Maxwell and Brian Clough.

I had in fact spoken to both Derby and Forest before my spell of
French leave, shortly after the season had ended. The Baseball
Ground had been my first port of call, where I enjoyed a simple
lunch with manager Arthur Cox and his assistant, Roy
McFarland. I was impressed by their obvious enthusiasm for the
game, but remained unconvinced about Derby's ability to compete
with the best. I was even less convinced when I received their offer
of terms.

A few days later I was again on my travels, this time to the City
Ground, Nottingham, to meet the one and only Brian Clough. I
was having talks with Watford later that day, so I decided to spend
the weekend in London with my future wife, Leslie. We arrived at
the ground and were shown to a lounge area by chief scout Alan
Hill.

Ten minutes later 'Cloughie' entered wearing his familiar green
goalkeeper top and tracksuit bottoms. He greeted Leslie with a
kiss, and said, 'Hello my beauty' in his highly distinctive and
much-mimicked drawl. Then he turned to me: 'Let me shake your
hand.' He shook it and backed off. There was a pregnant pause

ABOVE LEFT My father in his playing days for Lincoln. He scored over 200 goals before turning to football management

ABOVE RIGHT When I joined Arsenal, the world was at my feet . . . or so I thought

BELOW A happy start to my professional career at Stoke – before things turned sour

ABOVE LEFT After Arsenal . . .
a brief spell at Sunderland –
more of the same

ABOVE RIGHT My move to
Sheffield Wednesday heralded
happier times – here taking a
tumble in a game against
Arsenal

RIGHT Chelsea are the
opponents this time. My four
seasons at Hillsborough
enabled me to re-establish
myself in the First Division

Determination and a little help from my friends kept me out of Robert Maxwell's clutches. 'We'll get you out of there, hold tight,' said Brian Clough. And with Nottingham Forest I reached Wembley at last – twice. A wonderful feeling – parading the Simod Cup after scoring the last-minute winner against Everton

ABOVE A few weeks earlier we had beaten Luton 3–1 in the Littlewoods Cup Final

BELOW Signing for Leeds and rejoining Howard Wilkinson – a combination of club and manager that persuaded me to move down to the then Second Division

ABOVE The *coup de grâce* in an exhilarating away performance at Aston Villa

BELOW LEFT At 31 I'm selected for the England B team, 11 years after winning an Under-21 cap – I always have been a late developer!

BELOW RIGHT Not a car crash but the aftermath of the 1991 away game against Spurs. My little boy was afraid to come near me and plastic surgery was required!

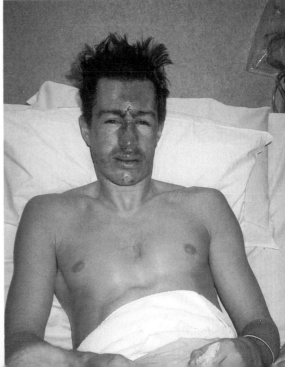

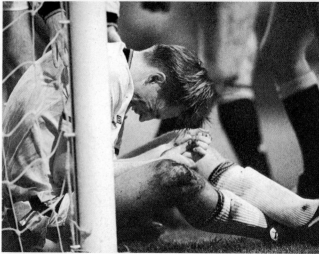

TOP AND CENTRE
The FA Cup defeat
against Manchester
United in January
'92 was memorable
for the wrong
reasons. This
spectacular header
which I was
convinced would be
the equaliser (but
which went wide)
resulted in a heavy
fall and a badly
broken wrist

BOTTOM I didn't play
again until the end
of February. The
apprehension evident
in my comeback
game against Luton
was unfounded – we
won 2–0, I scored
one of the goals
(Eric Cantona the
other) and came
through unscathed

ABOVE AND BELOW LEFT Another great feeling – parading the Championship trophy at Elland Road in our final game, and the game before at Sheffield United that made it all possible

BELOW RIGHT A great start to the new campaign – celebrating our Charity Shield win against Liverpool at Wembley

ABOVE Our first game in the new Premier League – we beat Wimbledon 2–1. Unusually, I got off to a flier with two goals, including this 86th-minute winner

BELOW David Batty, Eric Cantona and I begin to celebrate the Championship win. It was the first of many bottles of champagne that night!

and then he said, 'I want to shake your hand again', which he duly did. It was all very unnerving. We had just sat down when he asked: 'How old are the two of you?' We were both twenty-eight. He turned to Leslie, 'You've shot it!', then to me, 'You've shot it! You two get married, and you come and play for me.' A brief, awkward conversation followed until I was summoned into an office to discuss terms alone with him.

The uncomfortable prospect of talking money was made even worse when Cloughie sat down and rolled his tracksuit bottoms up above his knees. It was a very off-putting sight. 'How much do you want?' he demanded. I told him. 'Fucking hell! You must be joking! I don't get paid that and I'm better than you.' He made his offer, which was an improvement on Derby's but was somewhat short of my demands. I said I would think about it and rejoined Leslie in the lounge. As we left I received a kiss from Cloughie on my cheek. 'Come and play for me. We'd love to have you,' he shouted as we left the room. I spent the journey down to Watford trying to work out what had happened to me.

We were met at Watford by manager Steve Harrison, later to become a coach for England under Graham Taylor. Brief talks were followed by an invitation to meet chairman Elton John after watching him perform at a Prince's Trust concert at the Albert Hall. As we sat in a private box, I suddenly realised that this was all a wooing ploy to offset the unfashionable image that the club had. After the concert we were taken to meet the chairman in his penthouse suite in the Inn on the Park in Park Lane. I knew this would not be a happy occasion, due to Elton's appearance on stage earlier that evening. He had made a guest appearance with Phil Collins only to find his keyboards and microphone were not working. After an embarrassing wait, he had stormed off stage looking extremely annoyed.

On our arrival at the suite, we were greeted by Elton's wife, Renate, and by his manager, John Reid. They ushered us in and offered us a glass of Louis Roederer Cristal champagne from one of many such bottles on ice. The suite was something else and far removed from anything I had ever stayed in. Renate wafted around as if in a dream world, the worries of Watford FC being the last thing on her mind. As expected, Elton was very subdued, but still quite sociable. I got the impression he was tiring of his duties as chairman, and was merely going through the motions. He promised to match the offer from Forest but he later remarked that although all the potential buys liked him, few eventually signed. This proved to be the case with me.

Instead I signed for Niort, a team I had never heard of, from a town of sixty thousand inhabitants in the Poitou Vendée Charentes region of France, two hundred and fifty miles from Paris and a million miles away from my idea of continental football. Like Crewe it was a major railway junction, a place that everybody passes through, but rarely stops at.

On the face of it, my decision to join this French Second Division outfit may have looked strange, but I had reached a point in my life when I felt my career was at a standstill in the English game. Only a move to Forest really appealed to me, but their offer of terms fell short of what I wanted. When, out of the blue, Niort's extremely lucrative offer came, it seemed the right thing to do.

I was told they had just been relegated from the First Division, and were determined to return immediately. Their affluent sponsors had given them the go-ahead to buy whichever players were needed, and it seemed that money was no object. A move abroad had always appealed to me. It was a chance to sample a different culture, learn another language, and in doing so broaden my horizons.

After two days of talks, the contract was signed and we prepared for three years of life in France. The only stumbling block came between Wednesday and Niort, who could not agree a fee for me. That would have to be decided by a UEFA tribunal at a later date.

Things started well, and although I had arrived two weeks into their pre-season training, I soon slotted in and began to score freely in their warm-up matches. The difference between the English and the French game was very apparent. The system of intricate build-up play adopted by all of their teams meant the pace of the game was very much slower than ours. Their play, although containing a high level of technical ability, seemed to lack the passion and commitment of the British style.

I also noticed a distinct lack of discipline among the French players. They could not be pinned down to a specific job, but liked to wander from their given position whenever the mood took them. Many had a volatile temperament, which would often manifest itself when things were not going well. On several occasions players got themselves sent off because of their inability to cope with a losing situation.

When I arrived in France, I barely spoke a word of the native tongue. This made life extremely difficult in the beginning, although one of the players, Pierre Maurice, who was married to an American and spoke reasonable English, proved invaluable as an interpreter. For the first frustrating weeks I did not understand any of the dressing-room conversation, until, bit by bit, I gradually picked up a modest understanding of the language. It is a strange feeling to be left out of every conversation, and it was an experience I remembered when Eric Cantona arrived at Leeds from Nîmes. With my basic knowledge of French, I tried to help Eric in the same way that Pierre Maurice had helped me.

Life at the club was entirely different from that at my previous ones. For a start I had to supply my own training kit, and wash it. Worse still, I even had to clean my own boots! The facilities were adequate and comparable to a Third or Fourth Division English club. The council-owned stadium was clean and up to date, but lacked atmosphere, and was very small. Not that it needed to be any larger considering the Crewe-like attendances the club attracted.

The training at Niort varied from the routine I had been accustomed to in England. The day after a match was not, as I had been used to, a rest day, but one where all players were required to undergo a thirty-minute run. A more acceptable change was the compulsory weekly massage which I soon got used to. Massage is an integral part of Continental football, and is highly regarded for its ability to maintain fitness and peak performance. This is a concept that British clubs have yet to grasp.

I tried hard to blend in with my surroundings, learn the language and adopt as many of their customs as possible. One I could not get used to was the players' habit of greeting everybody with a shake of the hand each day. This involved shaking the hands of over thirty people every morning – after three days I gave up.

Away from the ground, the French way of life was much more easy to accept. Food and wine have been a great passion of mine for many years and I had no problems adapting to their eating habits. Their standard of cuisine and wine-making is unequalled anywhere in the world. The quality of even the most basic of restaurants puts to shame many of our so-called superior establishments. We have so much to learn from the French in this respect.

Lunch is a leisurely three-hour experience, whereas dinner can last even longer. During our short stay in France, we made many friends in the restaurant trade. Even though our French was limited they always went out of their way to help us and make us feel welcome. As the situation at the club deteriorated, the distractions of these restaurants kept us going. My one great regret was that I did not stay in France long enough to understand fully the language of these people.

Some good did come out of our stay in France. My wife, Leslie, was expecting our first child when we moved there. Shortly after our arrival she fell ill and was in grave danger of losing the child. However, the medical care in France is second to none and immediate blood tests were taken to establish the nature of her illness. Fortunately, the French are pioneers in the detection and treatment of toxoplasmosis, a blood complaint that can result in the death of a foetus or its subsequent birth with severe disabilities, such as blindness and brain damage.

Leslie was diagnosed as suffering from the complaint and was treated accordingly. Within a few weeks the toxoplasmosis was under control and both mother and child were safe. As things stood in Britain, there was every chance it would have gone undetected, and in this respect we were extremely fortunate to be where we were.

As the season progressed the team's performances started to deteriorate. This may well have had something to do with the fact that fifteen members of the squad had not been paid their signing-on fees. I was among them and had repeatedly enquired about the late arrival of my money. This was not an easy process when nobody spoke English and I knew just a few words of French. When eventually I made myself understood, I was told it would be paid very soon. My main reason for being there was purely financial and now that the money was not forthcoming, my presence at this small-time club could not be justified. I had assumed that French clubs must be the same as their English counterparts. Everyone was paid in England – why should it be any different in France?

One by one, the signs that the club was fast running out of money became evident. Initially, all away venues had been reached by air. France is a vast country and we were later to find out that this form of travel was essential. After a few weeks the journeys once taken by air were undertaken by road. This often resulted in horrendous ten-hour coach journeys to our away destinations. Games in France are played in the evening and we would often set out in the early hours of the day of the match. We would reach our venue, play, and immediately return home, arriving at seven o'clock the following morning. It was the most gruelling of schedules and it was no wonder the team's away form deteriorated rapidly.

The last match we travelled to by air was one I shall not forget in a hurry. We were to play Bastia on the island of Corsica, in the stadium that suffered the tragic stand collapse in May 1992, resulting in the loss of twelve lives.

I was reliably told by my colleagues that this was a game to be avoided. No professional in France relished the prospect of playing at this tiny ground. Mafia influences on the island were second only to those on Sicily, and bribery and corruption were rumoured to be rife. Referees on occasions were known to turn a blind eye or give outrageous decisions for the home team. I listened, but thought it to be a typical footballers' tale, slightly exaggerated and embellished.

After ten minutes of the game, I had comprehensively changed my mind. I had been spat at, elbowed, punched and finally tackled so late and high I needed several stitches in a gashed shin. All these incidents had happened under the nose of the referee, but for some strange reason he had failed to see any of them. Meanwhile the home supporters were stamping and banging on anything they had around them. It was hard to believe that a crowd of less than ten thousand could make such a deafening noise. It was the most hostile stadium I have ever played in.

We trundled off the pitch having lost 1–0, and thinking that at least our ordeal was over. Both teams walked up the tunnel to the dressing rooms together. As we walked I glanced across at their players and saw hatred in their eyes. Seconds later, three of the Bastia players grabbed hold of me and started to pull me towards their dressing room. What they would have done once inside, I dread to think, but they certainly were not going to discuss tactics or the exchange rate. Just as I was expecting the worst, an armed gendarme appeared from nowhere to rescue me and escort me back to my Niort colleagues. Back in the safety of the dressing room, I suddenly wondered what the hell I was doing there – was it all really worth it?

Financial gain had been the motivating force behind my move to this obscure club. The first instalment of my signing-on fee was a month overdue, and any hopes I had of receiving it appeared to be fading rapidly. My repeated requests were fobbed off, each time with a different excuse. I was fast running out of patience with the club, and its officials. This situation was exacerbated by the circumstances surrounding our accommodation. I had agreed to move out of a comfortable hotel and into an apartment, but only on the understanding that our promised house would be available in two weeks. It was now six weeks later and there was still no sign of this arrangement changing.

I knew the situation would shortly come to a head. The UEFA tribunal was due to meet to decide my valuation. Niort would then have to pay Sheffield Wednesday the relevant fee. It was quite obvious that Niort were unable to pay, whatever price was fixed. The only solution then was to raise revenue by selling me.

The UEFA tribunal arrives at the valuation of the player by a multiplication system which is based on the worth of a player's contract in his final year at his last club, and his age. The younger the player, the higher the multiplication factor. Wednesday had worked this figure out to be £325,000, whereas Niort valued me at £225,000. This discrepancy arose because of a dispute about a payment I had received at the beginning of my contract. As often happens in these cases, the difference was split and the fee was fixed at £275,000. For Niort I knew this was irrelevant – they could not afford to pay whatever the sum. Wednesday, on the other hand, were very unhappy with the whole process. If I had been transferred to an English club, they could have expected around half a million pounds more than they had demanded from the tribunal.

My subsequent transfer back to England for £400,000 a few weeks later exposed a loophole that could have been used by an unscrupulous club wanting to save money. If a club wanted to sign a player at the end of his contract and agreement could be reached with a European club who were prepared to act as a go-between, the player would move to the foreign club and the fee which would be set by the tribunal would be a fraction of the one decided between two English clubs. After a short period, the player would then be transferred back to England, to the club who had originally wanted him, for the same fee, or one that included a small facilities payment.

There were obvious advantages for any English club willing to use these methods. At the time Wednesday lodged a strong objection to my return. After consultation, the FA allowed the move to take place, but brought in new regulations that stopped this procedure from ever being repeated.

Immediately I had heard news of UEFA's tribunal ruling, I knew my return to England was inevitable. I saw the club secretary the following day and confronted him with my suspicions. To his credit, he admitted, for the first time, that the club were in serious financial difficulties and that they could not afford to pay my transfer fee. He then said that they would have to sell me and asked if I knew of any clubs in England who might want me. I told him I had talked to several before my move to France and I was sure they would still be interested.

As I left his office to return to our apartment, I had only one club in mind – Nottingham Forest. I had wasted the last three months of my career and that was enough. The débâcle of my move to Niort had taught me the importance of being with the right club. Money was important, but money alone was not enough. I had to be with a club that was involved at the top level, and was capable of winning trophies. I had endured the last three months playing in meaningless matches at substandard stadia, in front of paltry crowds. It had made me appreciate everything the English First Division had to offer, and how I needed to return to the team who could best satisfy my need for success – Forest.

Once inside the apartment I immediately telephoned Forest chief scout Alan Hill at his home. Shortly before my move to Niort I had telephoned Alan to tell him of my intentions. He had thanked me for calling and told me to give him a call if things did not work out. I was now doing just that. His wife answered and told me that Forest were at St Andrews in Scotland, enjoying a short break. She gave me the number of the hotel where they were staying and I spoke to Alan, who told me that Forest were still very interested. By a stroke of coincidence, the agent Denis Roach was present in Alan's room. Denis was a UEFA representative and also fluent in French. He had worked for Forest on previous occasions. Denis proceeded to call the Niort secretary who confirmed I was for sale. Forest then faxed the club informing them that they were willing to pay the transfer fee that Niort were asking for me.

The following day I received a call from the London-based agent, Eric 'Monster' Hall, so called because of his constant use of the word. I had dealt with him previously on a few occasions, but was surprised by his call and asked him where he had obtained my number. He had somehow extracted it from my sister, Denise, who was a photographic agent and had also worked with Eric. He was calling to let me know that Arthur Cox was aware of my situation and was still very keen to sign me. Although I had great respect for Arthur as a manager, I was well aware that Derby were in no position to challenge for any major honours. It was for this reason I had decided to contact Forest. I explained the situation to Eric and asked him not to give my number to Arthur under any circumstances. I had made my decision and it would only complicate matters if he did. He agreed and we said goodbye.

Ten minutes later the phone rang, and, surprise, surprise, Arthur Cox was on the other end – an amazing coincidence! I told Arthur I had contacted Forest and that I had made up my mind to sign for them. He asked me to listen to what he had to offer, and out of respect for him I heard him out. Nevertheless my mind was unchanged.

That evening, Brian Clough called. 'We'll get you out of there, hold tight,' he said. 'Do you want to play for me?' I said I did. 'Well, if you do, just stick by your guns, be strong and everything will be all right.' The call was short and to the point.

I knew my transfer back to Forest was going to be complicated, but little did I know just how complex the move would become. I had by now ceased to play for Niort and was training on my own. It all seemed so pointless and I longed to return to England, but I knew that would be impossible for a little while yet.

During the following days it seemed I was never off the phone. I was contacted by several clubs who were interested in buying me. Each time I listened, but politely declined every offer. One day I returned home from a lonely training session to find that Arthur Cox had been involved in a long conversation with Leslie. He had said they needed Leslie on their side if they were to have any chance of signing me. His conversation was very philosophical: 'People think the grass is greener on Forest's side of the motorway, but it isn't, the grass on this side has never been greener. Their flowers have bloomed, while ours are just about to blossom . . .' and so it went on. It seemed that Arthur was not going to give up – or that somebody would not let him give up.

An hour later, Peter Shilton, the Derby and England goalkeeper, was the next to call me. He sounded slightly embarrassed and had obviously been asked to speak to me by his manager. Peter, ironically a former Forest keeper under Clough, tried to persuade me to join Derby, and I listened politely to all he had to say. To save him further embarrassment, I kept the conversation to a minimum and thanked him for calling.

It was not long before Arthur called again. This time I spoke to him and my message got through. I told him of my respect for him as a manager, but emphasised that my decision to join Forest was made entirely for football reasons – Forest were capable of winning honours and Derby were not. Although he was disappointed, he said there were no hard feelings and wished me good luck.

The phone rang again. I picked it up and found I was talking to an 'Ian Maxwell from Derby'. He told me that an agreement had been made with the French club and that there were no barriers now to my return – but only if I signed for Derby. He added that somebody would be in touch and ended the conversation. I was totally unaware of whom I had been talking to. I had assumed it was a secretary from the club updating me on the latest situation. I was obviously aware of his father, Robert, the chairman of Derby and the head of the Maxwell business empire, but I failed to make the connection between the two. The call had been short and to the point and had taken me by surprise. I had assumed that it was Arthur who would not take no for an answer – how wrong I was.

An hour later my wife called me to the phone. 'It's Robert Maxwell!' she said, holding her hand over the receiver. A big grin lit up her face and I knew exactly how she felt – everybody else had called, so why not Robert Maxwell? 'Are you sure?' I whispered. She was.

'Robert Maxwell here, chairman of Derby,' were his first words, in that unmistakable, booming voice. 'Hello, Mr Maxwell,' was my humble reply. 'My manager tells me that you are a good player and he would like to sign you. Have you discussed terms with him?' I said I had, but had decided to join Nottingham Forest instead. He was undeterred. 'Well, I am calling to see if there is anything I can do. I understand you are in dispute with the French club over your contract.' I said I was. 'I will guarantee that your contract is paid up in full, in cash and into any overseas bank account you so desire. The French club are very keen to do business with me. I can be of great help to them through my many companies in Europe. Is there anything else you need?' I decided to go along with the game. 'A car,' I replied. 'What is your favourite car?' he demanded. 'A BMW,' was my answer. 'I have a fleet of BMWs. What model and colour would you like?' I stupidly replied, 'Red.' It was heady stuff.

He did not stop there, but moved on to Leslie. 'I understand your wife is an actress.' I confirmed she was. 'I own a satellite music station called MTV and I could guarantee her a job on that as a presenter. Have you seen our new *Sunday Mirror* magazine?' I told him I had heard about it. 'Well, it is better than any of its rivals and I will get her a couple of double-page features in that as well.' He went on condescendingly, 'Listen, I can tell you are not a typical thicky footballer. I can have my private jet sent over immediately and you will be back in England by tonight. Think the offer over and call me back in twenty minutes.' He gave me his private number at the Mirror Group offices in London and put the phone down abruptly without another word.

I talked the offer over with Leslie, but we both decided I should refuse it. I knew I was turning down a small fortune, and in fact that pleased me greatly. Even the power and affluence of Robert Maxwell had not turned my head. You always hope you will stick to your principles, but you never know for certain until the moment you are tested.

Thirty minutes lapsed before the phone rang again. It was Robert Maxwell wanting to know my decision. I thanked him for his offer and for his personal involvement, but told him that I had not changed my mind and would be joining Forest. He seemed stunned and after a short pause, he spoke. 'I think you are making a big mistake, but I wish you good luck.' With that he put the phone down.

I genuinely believed that would be the end of Derby's interest. I had been approached separately by both the manager and the chairman and had turned both down. What I had not taken into account was the added dimension this transfer wrangle had acquired. There was no doubt that both Derby and Forest wanted to buy me for my ability as a player, but now things had changed. The involvement of Robert Maxwell had transformed a fight between two clubs into a personal conflict between Maxwell and Brian Clough. Maxwell had run something of a campaign against Clough and Forest in an attempt to establish Derby as the premier club in the East Midlands, and it was common knowledge that there was no love lost between the two.

Stuart Webb, Derby's managing director, was the next to call. What he had to say was incredible, and only made me even more determined to join Forest. He informed me that a contract with Niort had already been signed and that I had to join Derby because Niort would not do business with anybody else. I was in effect being told that I had no say in the matter and would have to do as I was told. The conversation became heated as I grew increasingly annoyed at his stance. If there had been a slight chance of my joining Derby before this call, there was none now.

On Tuesday, 20 September, Alan Hill and Denis Roach arrived at Niort and a meeting was arranged with the club officials. We were kept waiting for almost three hours, and when the vice-president and secretary eventually turned up, we were told that the president, Pierre Figari, had already struck a deal with Derby County for my transfer. They intimated that they had already received money from them. I intervened and said that Niort had overlooked the most important point in this matter – they had not consulted Lee Chapman. I informed them there was absolutely no chance of my joining Derby. They seemed to accept my position and arranged for us to meet the president later that day.

We returned to the apartment in time to receive yet another call. My wife picked up the phone and found Brian Clough on the other end. 'Hello, my beauty. How are you?' he enquired. 'Oh I'm fine. Do you want to talk to Lee?' she replied. 'Do I heck! What do I want to talk to him for? It's you I want to speak to. Now, are you nice and warm?' Two days later a bouquet arrived for Leslie from Brian Clough and his family. On it was the message: 'Hope you're nice and warm.' This was my first insight into the way Cloughie operates. He makes a point of charming the players' wives so that they are on his side. He is then free to give the players hell knowing full well that any complaints about their treatment will not receive a sympathetic ear at home.

We arrived in good time for our 8.30 p.m. meeting with the president. Monsieur Figari eventually arrived at 12.30 a.m., four hours late. There was no apology. In matter-of-fact tones he told us that a deal with Derby had already been signed after a meeting with Ian Maxwell and Stuart Webb. This therefore meant I would be signing for them.

I was incensed. Not only had this man prevaricated consistently about my signing-on fee, but he now had the audacity to tell me who I would be playing for. After my disastrous three months in France, this really was rubbing salt into the wound. Not only was I extremely annoyed about the deal with Derby, but also with the shabby treatment I had received from Niort. Not once had I been approached by an official of the club to see how I felt about the situation.

I told him that I would only sign for Nottingham Forest and that if he would not allow me to do so, I would remain in France as a Niort player. His mood changed at this revelation. I knew he had to sell me to enable the club to survive, and the thought of me remaining at Niort had the desired effect. He arranged to meet us the following day after first speaking to Robert Maxwell.

The following morning the president agreed that the deal with Forest could go ahead – on one condition: I would have to speak to Derby once again. If my mind was still unchanged I could do as I chose. Stuart Webb was on his way over to Niort at that moment and it was arranged that I would meet him later that day.

At our meeting in the plush surroundings of the Niort board-room, Webb was immediately on the defensive after our stormy conversation on the phone. He asked if we could act like adults and start afresh. I agreed and listened to his offer – basically the one I had received from Robert Maxwell, with a few improvements thrown in. He asked me to think it over and phone him at the Derby ground two days later, directly after Saturday's home game. He gave me the number of the Derby boardroom and we parted company.

I had only attended this meeting to enable my deal with Forest to go ahead. For some reason, Stuart Webb must have read the situation incorrectly and assumed I would be signing for his club. In the Saturday edition of the Maxwell-owned *Daily Mirror*, the back-page lead proclaimed victory for Derby over Forest in the race for my signature. It also claimed that Brian Clough had 'bungled' the move by sending his 'office boy' Alan Hill to conduct talks instead of going himself.

Later that day, I called Stuart Webb, as agreed, to give him my decision. He seemed stunned at the news and reacted angrily, saying that Derby held my registration and I would not be able to play for another English club because they had signed a contract with Niort. After the morning's headlines, he must have felt very embarrassed indeed. Nevertheless, this was no excuse for making what I took to be a threat.

Pierre Figari had manoeuvred himself into a very difficult situation. He had signed a deal with Derby only to find it impossible to honour because of my refusal to sign for them. He had now agreed to transfer me to Forest, leaving him the problem of how to back out of his initial deal. He was due to meet Robert Maxwell in Maxwell's Paris office on the Wednesday, supposedly to finalise the move. It was such a daunting task that he insisted both Denis and Alan be there as well.

At this point there was no reason for me to remain in France any longer. My wife flew home with Denis and I drove our car back with Alan. Technically I was still a Niort player, but I had gone through enough and so I left without informing them. It was only how they had treated me.

That Wednesday, Denis and Alan flew to Paris and travelled to the arranged meeting place. It was a hotel directly opposite the Maxwell offices. Figari was to meet Robert Maxwell first and then go straight to the hotel. When the Niort president arrived, he was visibly shaken. He had the vice-president and treasurer in tow and said that he had been involved in a heated discussion. Robert and Ian Maxwell had both been present and were extremely unimpressed with the latest developments.

On hearing that I was unwilling to move to his club, Robert Maxwell was prepared to go to extraordinary lengths to prevent me from joining Forest. First he offered to give Niort approximately half a million pounds to keep me in France for the full three years of my contract. When this offer was refused, he attempted to buy the club outright. Niort would have joined a long list of clubs that Maxwell had owned, part-owned or tried to buy. Those clubs included Derby, Reading, Oxford, Watford, Manchester United and Tottenham Hotspur. I would in effect have become his property and been in a position where I could only go where he wanted me to go. The president had also refused this offer. He was only too aware that the sale of the club would have resulted in Maxwell installing his own people, a move that would have meant the end of Figari's presidency.

I could not believe that someone would be prepared to take such measures merely to get his own way. My feelings were of no significance whatsoever and he would have kept me at Niort against my will for three years. It would have been a severe abuse of power, simply to satisfy his oversized ego, though my own experience pales into insignificance in the light of the revelations which followed Robert Maxwell's death in 1991. Funnily enough, Niort were relegated from the French Second Division for financial irregularities that year, so perhaps they would not have made such strange bedfellows.

Although the odds were heavily stacked against us, we had stood up to Maxwell and beaten him. Denis Roach's ability to communicate in French had been vital, but the attitudes of Maxwell and Stuart Webb had made us even more determined in our efforts. I had been treated as though I was a piece of meat that could be bought and sold at will. I believed it was a severe abuse of my individual right of freedom of choice. The whole episode spoke volumes for Maxwell and Webb's opinions of professional footballers as a whole, or maybe they just treated everybody in that manner.

My transfer from Niort to Forest had been agreed but the situation was far from resolved. Niort had first to pay Wednesday the £275,000 the UEFA tribunal had decided upon. Now they had agreed a fee of £400,000 with Forest, they could obtain interim finance to settle their debt. At this point the issue was complicated by Wednesday objecting to my move back to England, on the grounds that Forest could have orchestrated the whole episode in order to purchase me for a reduced fee.

Yet again I was in limbo, but this time I could at least enjoy the comforts of my home in Sheffield, which we fortunately had not yet sold. At one time, there was a serious doubt about my registration with Forest, but eventually, after a period of four weeks, the problem was resolved.

In the meantime, it was vital I continued my training. I was unable to train with Forest, so an alternative club would have to be found. Obviously it would be impossible for me to train with my old club, Wednesday, so the local alternative, Sheffield United, were approached and Dave Bassett kindly allowed me to train with his first-team squad. It was a strange experience training with a team that I had no chance of being selected for. Training is always geared to Saturday's game, which is something all professionals look forward to. I was undergoing all the preparations for a match, with none of the sense of fulfilment from actually playing in one.

The spirit among the United players was obviously good. Although Dave Bassett was one of the few managers to be called by his Christian name, this did not stop him from commanding respect. Normally managers insist on being called 'Boss' or 'Gaffer', as a sign of deference. This did not seem to bother Dave, or 'Harry' as he had been affectionately known since his days at Wimbledon.

Although the training was enjoyable I did suffer a minor setback when, falling heavily, I broke one of the fingers of my left hand.

The bottom part of the finger was at right angles to the top and required a resetting and pinning operation. I was surprised how little pain I suffered. I was to be less lucky just over three years later, when I fell while playing for Leeds in that FA Cup tie against Manchester United.

When I finally got the clearance to sign for Nottingham Forest, I was more than ready to enter the fray of First Division football. I had not realised how addictive life in our top League had been. It had started to dawn on me during my spell in France, and now after six weeks without a competitive match, following three months of Second Division French football, I was positively desperate for a 'fix'.

My first game for Forest was for their reserves. Strangely enough, the match was against Leeds United at Elland Road, in front of a few hundred people. Not for one moment did I imagine I would be playing here, fifteen months later, in the colours of Leeds and in front of packed houses. My only thought at that time was to succeed at Forest. Their style of play was different from any at my previous clubs, and I knew it would not be easy. Nevertheless, I made a scoring debut in a comfortable win. Now I had to wait to see if I would be making my first-team debut at the Lions' Den, home of Millwall, three days later.

· 7 ·

The Clough experience

For weeks my career had been up in the air. Now I had joined a team renowned for playing the ball along the ground in short, swift passing movements, where players were expected to be comfortable on the ball in the tightest of situations. My move to Nottingham Forest was going to be challenging in more senses than one.

Before my move to France, I had been used exclusively as a traditional target man, required only to lay the ball off simply, and win anything in the air. During my short time with Niort, I had been forced to change my style somewhat in order to adapt to the slow build-up game favoured by French teams. The play of Niort mirrored that of Forest to some degree, except that it was not as accomplished. Now I would have to improvise to an even greater extent.

I was thrust into first-team action only a week after my arrival at the City Ground. It had been a nerve-racking debut at Millwall. Cold Blow Lane seemed the very antithesis of grounds like Anfield and Old Trafford, the type of venue to which I had been longing to return. The game finished a 2–2 draw, with Steve Hodge, a future colleague of mine at Leeds, scoring both goals. Things seemed to have gone quite well, but I was not certain until the manager shouted: 'Son, you did enough today.'

Every player has a honeymoon period when he first joins his new club. I knew that mine might even be slightly extended, due to my loyalty to Forest during the transfer wrangle. After that, like all players, I would be judged purely on merit, and my previous good acts would count for nothing.

Life at the City Ground was different from that at any of my previous clubs. I have never known a club, before or since, so dominated by one person. Admittedly, Forest are not the largest of clubs, but Brian Clough's presence seems to be in every part of the ground. He is held in awe by everybody, from board level down to the ground staff. It seems hard to imagine the club existing without him. Far from being an ever-present at the City Ground, however, he instead rationed his appearances and some weeks would not be seen until the Thursday or the Friday. When he was around, the difference in atmosphere was quite remarkable. Training suddenly acquired a fiercely competitive edge.

Players reported for training at 10.30 a.m. and then changed into their training gear. After a few cups of tea, the whistle would blow from the coaches' room, and off we would all go on our journey to the training ground. We reached the pitch by way of a leisurely stroll alongside the River Trent. It was at this point that we would find out whether the manager was present or not. If he was, one of the apprentices would be walking his pet dog, Del, at the front. Del invariably accompanied his master to the ground, and always watched us train.

Training never altered during my whole time at the City Ground. It would start with a running warm-up, often taken by captain Stuart Pearce. This was then followed by a brief session of sprints over short distances. These were always won by either Franz Carr or Des Walker, who unfortunately for us never seemed to be exerting themselves in doing so. Training finished with a short game of six-a-side, and then it was a walk back to the ground. The walk was often longer that the training sessions. Cloughie's great belief is that a player should not leave any energy on the training field, but save it for Saturday's game.

On our return to the dressing room, one of the players would go into the physiotherapist's room and take out of his fridge a large box of iced lollies, which were then handed out to everybody. These were brought in by Cloughie from one of the newsagent's shops he owned.

This was the routine to which we adhered during my stay at Forest, and which had been the same for many years before my arrival. The constant playing of six-a-side football is a major reason why Forest players look so assured in possession. It encourages players to improve their touch and feel for the ball in a pressurised situation. I personally was to benefit greatly from this over the ensuing months.

Another great change from my experiences at other clubs was

the total absence of any set-piece rehearsals. Not once did we rehearse a dead-ball situation When you have someone like Stuart Pearce to take free kicks, such practice tends to become irrelevant.

When the manager was not present, Liam O'Kane, the first-team coach, was in charge of training. Liam, a former Forest and Northern Ireland defender, was also required to run to the aid of any ailing player during first-team matches. For some reason, Cloughie would not allow physiotherapist Graham Lyas to carry the magic sponge and it was left to Liam to diagnose and treat any injuries. The manager seemed to have been deeply affected by his own tragic injury, which had prematurely finished his career at Sunderland in 1964. I'd heard he loathed hospitals and was not known to visit any injured players when they were recovering in one. He also disliked seeing any player on crutches at the City Ground.

Another of the backroom staff was the assistant manager, Ron Fenton. Ronnie seemed to be more of an ever-present at Cloughie's side than his dog, Del. He was definitely the manager's right-hand man in every sense and would fill in for him during his periods of absence from the ground. Archie Gemmill, the former Scottish international, was reserve-team coach, and by all accounts was a very hard taskmaster with a cutting sense of humour to match. He was not afraid to speak his mind, even to the manager. It was no surprise to hear that the two had been involved in several bust-ups, although they continue to work together at Nottingham with Archie now involved at first-team level.

Completing the set-up was chief scout Alan Hill, who had done so much to enable my transfer to Forest to take place. Alan, an ex-Forest number one, was often seen on the training ground taking specialist sessions for the goalkeepers.

The one thing that all the staff had in common was the unmistakable knowledge of who was boss. On several occasions, they would all be involved in a training session, when the shout from Cloughie would echo around the training ground: 'We're all in!' Immediately everybody – first team, reserves, and juniors – would stop and return to the ground.

Not only does the manager believe in plenty of rest for his players, he is also a great family man and is keen for his men to spend as much time with their families as possible. He therefore gives his players numerous days off, especially during the latter part of the season. I sometimes felt I was getting too much time off, but I blindly accepted it as part of the Cloughie way.

Reporting time for matches was always left as late as possible. I had been used to reporting for a pre-match meal three and a half hours before the start of the game. Now at Forest I was required to arrive at the ground only forty-five minutes before the kick off. Away trips were treated in just the same manner. Where possible, the travelling would be done on the day of the match, or, if an overnight stay was essential, arrival at the hotel would be shortly before the players' bedtime.

At home matches, we players would not see the manager until shortly before kick off. He was not one to mingle with his men as they prepared for the match. His was a dramatic entrance, intended to have the impact it always did. There were no great speeches, just little orders given to those he felt needed them. When I first arrived my message game after game was the same: 'Turn with the ball, that's what you're paid for! If you get hurt turning with it, that doesn't matter. That's what you get paid for!'

One of his favourite exercises just before we left the dressing room to run out on the field was to sit everybody down. He would then tell one of the coaches to place a ball in the middle of the dressing-room floor. 'Look at it!' he would order us. 'That's what you play with. Now go out there and PLAY with it! Go and win playing football.' There were never any tactical discussions or any talk of the opposition. His players know they are expected to control the ball and then pass it to one of their own team, preferably one in a forward position. The midfield and the forwards in particular know they are required to receive the ball and turn with it and the defenders know they must prevent the opposition from scoring. It sounds so simple – and it is. It has worked for Brian Clough for many years, and it will continue to do so for as long as he feels he can stay in football.

His ability to read a game is another of his great assets. If need be, minor adjustments are made either at half-time or during the match, often with devastating effect. His half-time talks are rarely overanimated and only ever begin when everybody has been sitting down for a few minutes and has had time to collect their thoughts.

The one major exception to this was during the half-time interval of a home reserve match, shortly after I had joined the club. The manager was far from pleased with his strikers that evening, especially Nigel Jemson, who was later to move to Sheffield Wednesday. Nigel, who was young and still learning, was having various disagreements with the coaches. All the players were sitting down with their heads bowed low, after a disappointing first half. Cloughie approached Nigel, and stood directly in front of him. 'Stand up!' he commanded. Nigel obediently stood up. 'Have you ever been hit in the stomach, son?' he enquired. As soon as Nigel had said 'No', Cloughie delivered a forceful blow to his midriff. Nigel doubled up in pain and let out an agonised groan. 'Now you have, son!' and with that he turned away.

After-match comment was usually kept to a minimum. If a player had performed badly, he would have been substituted and any rebuke was therefore unnecessary. A poor showing was not the only reason for the dreaded sight of your number being held aloft. One particularly bad pass might be all that was needed for the manager to replace you. If he particularly disliked anything that you had done, that was it: you were off.

Forest players are notorious for not giving after-match quotes to the waiting hordes of pressmen. They take their lead from the manager whose policy it is not to do so. He seems to have a deep distrust of journalists and speaks to them only on his terms. This distrust is common among most footballers, many of whom have been let down by one or more reporters at some stage in their careers. It is generally the tabloids, with their tendency to 'twirl' the most innocent remark, who have most to answer for in the development of this situation, although there has been an improvement in relationships of late. This is mainly because of the more responsible attitude developed by the editors – and because of the reluctance of many players to see their casual comments distorted into a 'shock, horror' headline.

My honeymoon period at Forest lasted only eight games, in which time I had scored just one goal. I then received a critical outburst from Clough in the popular press on the morning of our home game against Middlesbrough. It appeared I would not be selected and I waited nervously for the side to be announced. The players at Forest are only informed of the team about forty-five minutes before the kick off. Liam O'Kane will arrive in the dressing room and let the relevant players – those who have been dropped or promoted – know of their fate.

My relief at retaining my place was enormous. It was so great that I went on to score twice in a 2–2 draw. This seemed to be my turning point, and more goals soon followed as I became more comfortable in the team. After a quiet start to the 1988-89 season, results were picking up and we were still left in all the Cup competitions.

Two games later, during a fourth-round Littlewoods Cup replay, I scored to put us 2–1 ahead of Leicester. To my amazement, ten minutes later I was substituted. Cloughie was known to have a policy of never bringing off a goalscorer and I wondered why this had changed now. I walked forlornly over to the bench and sat down to watch the remainder of the match. A few minutes later the manager asked me: 'Who got the goal, by the way?' I told him it was me. 'Oh, I didn't realise,' was his response. It was the only time I was ever aware of his missing anything during a game.

Our next match in the Littlewoods Cup was the quarter-final tie at home to Queen's Park Rangers. It turned out to be my finest performance in a Forest shirt, as I scored four times in a 5–2 victory. It was the greatest number of goals I had scored in one match, and as I walked into the dressing room I felt sure of a great reception from the manager. 'Eh, Chapman!' he shouted. 'When you score a hat trick, you run over to me, not the supporters. I'm the one who signed you!' It was typical Clough. Just when you expect one thing, you get the exact opposite. Despite the manager's rebuke, my spirits were still very high. My display was significant in that it had proved conclusively I had adapted to the Forest style of play. I looked forward to some favourable headlines the following morning.

I should have known better. There was hardly a mention of my career-best goalscoring performance. Instead Cloughie had grabbed the headlines in all of the papers. There had been a small after-match pitch invasion by a few home supporters, and the manager had been incensed by their action. In an attempt to remove them, he had struck two of them around the head. His actions had been caught by the television cameras and it seemed disciplinary action by the Football Association and the police was inevitable. That may have been the case with anybody else, but this was Brian Clough. Not only did he escape any punishment whatsoever, but the two supporters in question offered the manager unreserved apologies for being on the pitch in the first place! They received a televised kiss for their troubles.

His reaction to the invading supporters had been understandable. He has always been a strict disciplinarian, a fact that is reflected in the exemplary disciplinary record of his teams. The City Ground is his domain and he therefore expects the same standard of behaviour from the supporters as well. He had previously asked the crowd to refrain from swearing and has erected boards saying 'No swearing gentlemen – Brian'.

Every player in a Forest shirt is aware of the need for good behaviour on the field. It is something that is stressed to them by the manager on a regular basis. Any misdemeanours in this area are punished severely with heavy fines. Cloughie is in many ways a father-figure to his players and in this respect he has his greatest influence on the younger members of the club. As players get older, however, some of the more individually minded can tire of his parental guidance. As a twenty-nine-year-old, with a wife, child and large mortgage, I found it very strange when walking out of the toilets to be asked by the manager if I had washed my hands.

A strong character who has been able to work with Cloughie for many years is captain Stuart Pearce. 'Pearcey' is the dominant personality at Forest, both on and off the field, the manager excepted, of course. His surging runs and never-say-die attitude are a constant encouragement to all of his team-mates. His style of play is further enhanced by his lethal strikes at free kicks. This and his emergence from non-League football, when he worked as an electrician, have combined to make him the undisputed crowd favourite, with the affectionate nickname of 'Psycho'. I know of many wingers who believe this nickname to be totally justified. They view their encounters with him with as much relish as a trip to the dentist.

Until recently Pearcey has had a rather sullen image, mainly due to his reluctance to speak to the press. Of late he has made an effort to be more co-operative, almost certainly in response to Graham Taylor's comments that his England captain must be able to deal with the media. In the company of his colleagues, however, the Forest skipper is a merciless mickey-taker, who spares no one from the cutting edge of his tongue. I have had many good times with him, but my one abiding memory is of a pre-season tour of Bordeaux. On a night off, Steve Hodge, Brian Rice, Pearcey and I decided to eat at a typically French restaurant. It had been a long and fruitless trip, so out of boredom we decided to have a 'French hour' in which nobody could talk unless they spoke in the native tongue. I spoke a little French from my time in Niort, but the others knew just a handful of words. It was very funny stuff, but the undoubted star of the show was Pearcey with his hilarious brand of cockney-franglais.

The one thing I do not miss about him is his taste in music. Pearcey is still a punk rocker at heart and lists the Clash, the Lurkers and the Buzzcocks as just a few of his favourite bands. I can take them in small doses, but Pearcey was the only one to remember to bring tapes on away trips. The Clash is fair enough, but a solid two hours of the Lurkers is more than anybody should be expected to endure.

As is typical of Forest in recent times, the second half of the season saw a dramatic improvement in form. Progress in the FA, Littlewoods and Simod Cups was trouble free, and our League position improved on a regular basis.

An FA Cup fourth-round tie saw a spirited Leeds United side fight us all the way at the City Ground. Their new manager, Howard Wilkinson, was obviously turning the team around and we were hard pushed to finish 2–0 winners. My volleyed goal which opened the scoring was a nice way to remind my old manager that I still had not lost the knack.

A narrow two-leg aggregate victory over Bristol City in the semi-final put us through to the final of the Littlewoods Cup against Luton on 9 April, a little over five months after I had joined the club. After eleven years as a professional, I was finally going to fulfil one of my ambitions – to play at Wembley in a cup final.

It was everything I had expected, and more. I soaked up the atmosphere and enjoyed every minute I was there. Ten minutes into the match, it seemed I had made a dream start when I scored from eight yards out. Unbelievably the referee blew for offside, although video evidence showed the goal to be a good one. Luton then went ahead, but a strong second half revival enabled us to finish comfortable 3–1 winners. It was the first medal of my career and one I had feared might never come. It certainly had not seemed possible just six months earlier in Niort.

Man of the match that day was Nigel Clough, the scorer of two of our goals. It must have been hugely satisfying for Nigel to shine on such a big occasion. More often than not, the team's performance was, and still is, very dependent on that of Nigel. The whole team is geared to him dropping back into the midfield and receiving the ball. From here he is able to deliver those defence-splitting passes that can cause so much havoc.

Nigel has coped admirably with an extremely difficult situation. It cannot be easy for any player to be in a team which is managed by his father. When that father is Brian Clough, the problem is many times greater. Father and son are quite a contrast. Nigel is quietly spoken and very unassuming. He is always the last to report for training and one of the first to leave afterwards. He changes quietly and rarely socialises with other players away from his work surroundings.

When father and son are together, and in front of the other players, communication is kept to a minimum. The manager usually refers to him as 'the centre forward', whilst Nigel, during my time at the club, spoke to his father only when spoken to. He has managed to overcome the awkward position with such success that it is hard to imagine him being anywhere but at the City Ground. Pisa were once keen to sign him, but according to Clough senior, Nigel's mother was having none of it.

The day after the Littlewoods final, I went for a celebratory lunch with eight of my family and friends. Ironically, in view of the transfer wrangle between the two East Midlands rivals, I now lived near Derby, and we had chosen to eat in a local restaurant. As we sat down at our table, we suddenly realised that the manager, who also lived nearby, was with his family on the other side of the room. He sent a message over saying that he hoped we would not be embarrassed by his presence, and before he left he came over to say hello to everybody. The lunch was a great success, especially now all at the table had met the great man. When it finally ended, we asked for the bill, only to be told that Cloughie had already settled it. When the mood took him, there was no one more generous.

Six days after our Littlewoods success, we were involved in another big game. This time it was the FA Cup semi-final against Liverpool at Hillsborough. It was an occasion I will never forget – but for the wrong reasons.

The game kicked off amid a crescendo of noise, with Forest playing towards the Leppings Lane End. Almost from the kick off, Peter Beardsley hit the bar and then we counter-attacked. I had received the ball wide on the right, just outside the penalty area, when suddenly the referee called a halt to the game. We were then told to leave the pitch because of crowd trouble. We were at first reluctant to go, but were ushered off by the police. We went back to the dressing room fully expecting to return to the field. There had been no obvious sign of any trouble and it seemed highly likely our wait would be short.

After half an hour we were told by an officer that the game would probably be abandoned, but no reason was given. I wandered out into the tunnel area to see if I could find out what was happening, only to witness chaotic scenes, with everybody rushing to and fro. I had spent four years at Hillsborough and I knew everybody by name. I spoke to Bob Gorrill, the Wednesday commercial manager, and asked him what was wrong. He had tears in his eyes as he told me how the club gymnasium was being used as a morgue, and how it was littered with bodies. He said that the Leppings Lane End gate had been opened by the police and the ensuing surge of people had caused those at the front to be crushed. I looked around at the familiar faces of the office girls; all of them had tears rolling down their faces.

I could not take it in. I was numb, but I immediately feared for the safety of my sister and her boyfriend who were present at the game. I finally found somebody who could assure me of their safety, and then I returned to the dressing room. When I broke the news to the manager that many of the Liverpool fans had died, he snapped: 'Don't tell me that!' Like me, he did not want to believe it.

We finally left Hillsborough at 6 p.m., and hardly a word was spoken on the trip back. When I arrived home, I relived the horror of the afternoon's events, firstly through the television coverage, and then through my sister and her boyfriend. They had been seated next to the Leppings Lane End and were forced to witness scenes that would stay with them for ever. The gruesome spectacle of life being extinguished had unfolded before them. It made the game of football seem very insignificant.

Two weeks later we had to put those tragic events to the backs of our minds. We were in yet another Wembley final. This time it was the much-maligned Simod Cup, and our opponents were Everton. It was a memorable final played in front of 47,000 supporters, the bulk of whom were from Nottingham. The game went to extra time before we finally won 4–3. I scored twice, including the last-minute winner, and it was yet another night of celebration, albeit somewhat muted.

Seven days later, we were expected, in the aftermath of Hillsborough, to play Liverpool in the replay of the abandoned FA Cup semi-final. For some strange reason, known only to the Football Association, it was decided that the competition should continue. It was a match that should never have been played. It was not fair to expect either team to compete again in the FA Cup after the events of that first game. For Liverpool, it became a crusade for those who had died. It seemed we were in an impossible position, and were there only to make up the numbers. The match finished 3–1 to Liverpool, but in effect the competition had ended at Hillsborough. It is a shame that the Football Association did not make it official, as the French Football Federation decided to do following the Corsican stand disaster in 1992.

It was then a matter of clearing the inevitable backlog of League fixtures. We had won thirteen of our final twenty games to finish third in the table. It had been a memorable campaign in many ways. Forest had become the first team to win two Wembley finals in a season, our League position equalled the club's highest since 1979 and we had reached the semi-finals of the FA Cup. Nevertheless, all this success was tinged with the sadness of the events of 15 April.

On a personal note, my two winner's medals had been immensely satisfying. Not only was I at last a winner after eleven years as a professional, but my decision to join Forest instead of Derby had been completely vindicated. There had been times during those complex negotiations when I wondered whether I was doing the right thing by turning down all the money and incentives that Robert Maxwell was offering me. Even during that initial period with Forest, when I was finding it difficult to settle in, I had doubts again. These were now but distant memories as I prepared for an enjoyable summer off.

The club, as usual, had organised an end-of-season trip to Cala Milor. This holiday resort in Mallorca had been a favourite of Cloughie's for many years. There was at least one trip there every year, either during or after the season. Before we left for our holiday all the wives received chocolates and magazines from the manager. After our Littlewoods and Simod Cup triumphs they had all received a bouquet with a message thanking them for all their help. Although it may have been a genuine thank you, it was also a brilliant psychological move which enabled Cloughie to get the wives firmly on his side.

The trip was a chance for players to unwind, have a few beers and swap a few stories. One day we were sitting on the front, soaking up the sun, when we spotted the manager and his entourage coming our way. He always seemed to have at least three of four of the staff with him at any one time. When he reached us, he stopped and asked if he could join us. We of course said yes, so he and his followers sat themselves down. Cloughie is not the type of man you can laugh and chat with over a drink, so conversation stopped the moment he arrived. As soon as he was seated, he pulled a paperback out of his pocket and began to peruse it. He read for fifteen minutes without uttering a word, until suddenly he got up and said, 'Thanks for your company, lads.' With that he left and the others followed.

During the week away many stories were related, most of them involving the manager. The tales had been passed down over the years and had almost become folklore. Larry Lloyd, who was Forest's centre half during the late seventies, features in several of the Clough anecdotes. Larry had won three England caps at Liverpool, but fell out of the international reckoning until he joined Forest. On his recall by Ron Greenwood, England were thrashed 4–1 by Wales. Shortly afterwards in the Forest dressing room, Larry was confronted by Cloughie. 'Larry, which England international got two caps on the same day?' Larry thought long and hard before saying: 'I don't know, boss. Who was it?' The reply was devastating: 'You did. Your fourth and your last!'

Another time, so the story goes, Forest had played an evening match in Greece and were now congregating in the hotel foyer before departing for the airport. Although the temperature was soaring, the manager had stipulated that everybody must report wearing the club blazer and slacks. The only one who did not conform was Larry, who was wearing a tracksuit. Cloughie instantly spotted him and shouted over: 'Go and get your blazer on!' Larry was adamant: 'No, it's too warm. I'm wearing my tracksuit.' The manager immediately replied: 'If you don't put it on, I will fine you £100.' The answer was defiant: 'I don't care.' 'Right, that's £100. If you don't put it on now, I'll double it.' Larry's only reply was 'Go on, then' . . . and so it went on. During the trip back, the fine was doubled many times over, until Larry reached home a much poorer man.

Another centre half from the same period was Kenny Burns, who went on to play for Leeds before moving into the pub business. Kenny had been warned many times about passing the ball square across the front of his own goal. During the second half of a subsequent match, he again defied the manager's orders and repeated the feat. The final whistle blew and Kenny walked back to the dressing room to find an envelope waiting for him at his changing place. He opened it: it was a typed letter on official club paper – he had been fined by the manager for disobeying orders.

As part of our pre-season training schedule for the 1989-90 season, we spent a week in France at Bordeaux's training camp. Unbelievably the manager was not present for any of the trip. Cloughie is the only manager I know who would have been absent at such a crucial time in his team's preparations. But this was his way; he was unpredictable and always kept his players guessing his next move. Throughout the whole of that week, we expected him to turn up at any time.

The start of the 1989-90 season saw another indifferent start from Forest. This had become something of a habit over recent years. The poor start is generally followed by an improvement around Christmas and a strong finish in the second half of the season. This late surge of form may go a long way to explaining why Forest usually do well in the Cup competitions, which are only resolved towards the end of the season.

One reason for this trend may be linked to Forest's training schedule. Pre-season training is very mild, compared with all the other clubs I have played for. When the season starts, most teams are physically better prepared, a fact that is borne out by Forest's poor start. Training during the season is also very relaxed, which means that players are only going to reach the peak of their fitness by playing in matches. By the time this is achieved, success in the League is usually beyond their reach, but all the Cup competitions are still undecided and wide open to any team still left in them. Although our League form was patchy, steady progress was made in the Littlewoods Cup.

After one home match that season, at which the ITV cameras were present, an interview was requested with winger Franz Carr. Franz had given a fine display and was the obvious candidate for the after-match talk. As always, the request was made via the manager.

Cloughie was in a frivolous mood and told the television people they could have their man in ten minutes' time. He immediately sent for a black apprentice and told him he would be doing the interview impersonating Franz Carr. The young lad had no option but to agree, even though he bore little resemblance to Franz. The prank seemed doomed to backfire, but unbelievably, the interviewer accepted him as the real thing. The cameras rolled and a full interview was given. Needless to say, when the truth was later discovered, those at ITV were far from happy.

Cloughie had a history of buying and selling players without giving them a game. He would also suddenly go off an established player for no apparent reason. Asa Hartford lasted just four weeks, while John Sheridan and Gary Megson were both signed for large sums of money, but then sold without being given a chance to prove their worth. Many of his signings are bought on the recommendation of either chief scout Alan Hill, or assistant manager Ron Fenton. There is a standing joke among the Forest players about this – you are either a 'Hilly' signing or a Fenton signing, and those signed by Fenton usually last longer than those signed by 'Hilly'.

I was at Forest during John Sheridan's short stay, and when I overheard the manager saying 'He can't fucking run,' I knew his days were numbered. Cloughie likes his midfield players to get up and down the field, whereas John's game was to 'sit' and distribute the ball. He also did not fit into the manager's concept of his players being neat and clean-shaven.

Gary Megson arrived at Forest late into pre-season training. Shortly after his arrival he travelled with the first team to a friendly game at Dundee. I had been with Gary at Sheffield Wednesday where I knew of his long-standing habit of making himself sick before a match and at half-time. Gary had played in the first half at Dundee and at half-time had gone into the toilets to go through his ritual. Cloughie came into the dressing room and heard retching noises coming from the toilets. 'What the hell is that noise?' he demanded. 'It's Meggy being sick,' answered one of the players. He called Gary back into the room. 'Why are you being sick?' he enquired. 'I'm always sick at half-time,' was Gary's reply. The manager's reaction said it all: 'Not in my dressing room, you're not!'

Gary never played in a first-team game again. So intimidating had the manager been that Gary, afraid to be sick in the dressing room, retched as he went on to the pitch for reserve-team matches. Not satisfied with this, the manager went on to describe Gary in the press as not being able to 'trap a bag of cement'. Gary reacted badly to this criticism, but to succeed with Cloughie, this sort of talk has to be taken with a pinch of salt. If you take it in your stride and go on to succeed, he respects you all the more. The one thing you cannot be with him is sensitive. Gary was, and that is why his stay at the City Ground was short-lived, although he has since been a consistent First Division performer with Manchester City.

One Forest player who definitely was not sensitive to criticism was Des Walker. Not that he received much. From time to time, the manager would accuse him of being a 'bighead' but this never once seemed to bother him. It was a term the manager had often used to describe himself.

Des's policy of never speaking to the press – not even after he finally broke his scoring duck during the 1991-92 campaign – has given him an image of not being a good talker. Although there were times when we wished this to be true, never can an image have been so far removed from reality. When Des is in full flow, it is difficult for anyone else in the dressing room to enter the conversation. Des is ultra-confident and even the constant ribbing he received about never having scored a goal during his career failed to bother him. The only player able to get to him was Stuart Pearce, who had the perfect put-down. Des's two prominent front teeth had earned him the nickname of 'Arkle' and the sound of Pearcey's horse impersonation was usually enough to do the trick.

As the season progressed my relationship with the manager started to deteriorate. He had suddenly gone off players before and now it appeared it was happening to me. He became more critical of me, despite the fact that I was the only player scoring goals on a regular basis. In mid-November, before our away match at Manchester United, he called me to him and said: 'I'm thinking of leaving you out today. What do you think?' My reply was predictable. 'I don't think you should.' He ended the brief conversation by saying that he would think about it. I had been pleased with my recent form and found this hard to take. Whether he meant it or whether he was trying to wind me up, I don't know, but either way it was not the way to motivate me.

The following game, at Manchester City, brought things to a head. At half-time he said he was not happy with my work rate. It was a statement that infuriated me. Endeavour has been the one thing I have not lacked throughout my entire career and it was the first time I had ever been accused of not giving it. I snapped back: 'Well, if you're not happy, go and get somebody else!' 'I will,' he replied. No one ever answers the manager back, and now that I had done it, I felt it was a turning point in my career at Forest.

Cloughie's management style is not based on players giving their opinions, but only on him imposing his. That is perfectly fine if you are able to work under those conditions, but I did have an opinion and the situation had become stifling.

Four games later, I was dropped for the visit to Luton. The fact that I was the leading scorer and had scored two goals in the last three matches, including one in the last game, might have counted for something with other managers, but not with Brian Clough.

I knew my time at Forest had now come to an end. My omission from the team and a financial problem unrelated to football necessitated my immediate transfer to another club. I sought a meeting with the manager and explained my situation. He was sympathetic and said he would allow me to leave if I really wanted to go. He asked me if I had another club in mind. I had been told by a source close to Elland Road that Leeds United were looking for a centre forward, and that their manager, Howard Wilkinson, would probably be interested. Contact between the two clubs was made and a fee was agreed.

The following day I reported to the manager before leaving for talks at Leeds. I was told by his secretary that he was busy, and I would have to wait outside his office. I had only been waiting a short time when Cloughie popped his head round the door and told me to come into his office. I walked in to find Gary Charles sitting in front of the manager's desk. Gary had made just two first-team appearances but was destined to gain full England honours the following season. The manager showed me to a chair in the corner. I assumed he had asked me in for a reason, so I sat down and listened.

To my amazement, I found myself in the middle of Gary's contract negotiations. Cloughie opened: 'So you think you are worth a new contract?' Gary was a shy lad at the best of times, so this situation must have been very intimidating for him. He answered meekly, 'Yes.' 'How much do you think you're worth?' asked the manager. 'I don't know,' was the reply. No one could have predicted the next question from Cloughie: 'Do you like vegetables, son?' Gary looked very puzzled as he admitted he did. 'Which ones do you like?' he was asked. Gary was stunned into silence. 'Do you like cabbage?' Cloughie continued. 'It's all right,' was the bewildered reply. 'What about Brussels sprouts?' 'Yes, I like them,' said Gary. 'Well then, do yourself a favour – go to the greengrocer and buy yourself a big bag of Brussels sprouts.' Gary looked totally bewildered and I felt for him. He was not the first player – and he would not be the last – to go through such an ordeal. It was all part of playing for Brian Clough. At this point, I felt I was intruding, so I got up and left the room.

Shortly afterwards Cloughie came out to me. 'Tell Leeds to piss off, and stay with us!' he said. 'I can't,' I replied. 'I've got to go.' 'All right,' he said. 'Good luck, and remember we're still friends.' With that he gave me a kiss and we parted – again, it was typical Clough, unpredictable to the last.

I had been with Forest for just fifteen months, but what a fifteen months it had been. I had been a winner at Wembley twice and had seen a vast improvement in my game – my touch had improved and, according to Archie Gemmill, I had turned with the ball more often in my time at Forest than I had during the whole of my career. Up until Forest most of my goals had been scored at the far post. Cloughie's insistence on crosses being played only to the near post had forced me to adapt and become a near-post forward. I knew that after I left Forest I could add this newly acquired ability to my repertoire.

I had been given the chance to work with one of the game's greatest managers and had gained a valuable insight into how he worked. It had been fascinating, but because of our strong personalities, it was never destined to be a long association. If I had been ten years younger, I might have been more ready to accept the Clough way or been moulded into accepting it, like so many of his youngsters. Nevertheless, I had always aspired to play for Brian Clough, and now I had done so, I felt enriched by the experience.

I often wonder what will become of Forest when Brian Clough decides to call it a day. Who will take over and will the club ever enjoy the success it has enjoyed during the Clough era? The answer to the latter question is that I very much doubt it. Cloughie has performed miracles in producing such success with the limited resources at his disposal. There is no doubt that he is a one-off and his like will never be seen again. But more than this, his domination of every aspect of the club is such that the transition period after his departure could be as painful and prolonged as the one Leeds endured after Don Revie left in 1974.

The problem of a replacement is a bit more difficult. I am sure there are members of the Forest 'boot room' who would love the job.

Assistant manager Ron Fenton may seem an obvious choice to an outsider, but my inside knowledge tells me he would not be the players' choice. Over the years too many players have felt they have been let down by him through his strong allegiance to the manager. It is a stigma that will not go away. Archie Gemmill, the reserve-team coach, would in many ways provide similarities to Cloughie. He is outspoken, forthright and at times abrasive. He has not been known to tell tales and in this respect he has proved to be his own man. He has been at the club long enough to know its workings inside and out, and he must be a candidate. First-team coach Liam O'Kane has always had a good relationship with the players and he too would come into contention. In fact a Gemmill/O'Kane partnership would in many ways be an ideal solution to the managerial position, if it became vacant.

My outside bet for the job was suggested to me by Steve Hodge shortly before I left Forest. At the time, everyone, including myself, dismissed his theory out of hand. In the meantime, I have changed my mind. The person in question has proved he has powers of leadership, he is a firm favourite with the supporters, and he has shown recently that he can handle the media: although it may be too early for Stuart Pearce at the present time, he will surely be in contention at some time in the future.

The choice, I am sure, will be influenced enormously by Brian Clough. He first has to make the decision to retire and I sincerely hope he does not leave it too late. The pressures of his job are very intense, as recent tragic cases have proved only too conclusively. I am sure that, whatever happens, he will always be used in a consultative role. Nottingham Forest without Brian Clough seems inconceivable.

· 8 ·

Now or never with Leeds

Life after Clough for me meant returning to play for Howard Wilkinson once again – this time in the Second Division. My transfer to Leeds meant I would have to play below the top level in England for the first time since my League debut with Plymouth. It was a move I would never have made but for the combination of club and manager.

It was common knowledge within the game that at the time Leeds were a very ambitious outfit. The buzz filtering through the grapevine was that the Leeds board were totally committed in their desire to return the club to the greatness of former years. After the anguish of eight years in the Second Division and the policy of appointing former players as manager – Allan Clarke, Eddie Gray and Billy Bremner were among the seven managers between the departure of Don Revie in 1974 and the arrival of Wilkinson in 1988 – Leeds had a radical rethink and appointed an 'outsider'. Ironically, their first choice had been Howard Kendall, but they had been unable to lure him from the Spanish club Athletic Bilbao. Who can say how the club would have fared if their attempt had been successful?

The board, on appointing their new manager, decided to remove the financial shackles that had restricted him in his previous employment at Sheffield Wednesday. He was now in a position to offer salaries that were better than most in the First Division. This factor certainly influenced my decision to drop down a division – albeit, I hoped, temporarily. The man who has been largely responsible for enabling these resources to become available is the chairman, Leslie Silver, who has injected large sums of his own money into the club, and has acted as guarantor for very much more. He has been ably assisted by Peter Gilman the vice-chairman

and by flamboyant managing director Bill Fotherby who has negotiated many successful sponsorship deals.

It was strange I should be signing for a team I had particularly
disliked as a child. During the Revie era of the late sixties and
early seventies, Leeds had been *the* team to hate. They were
renowned for being dirty, cynical and ruthless. To make matters
worse, they played the kind of football you wished your team were
able to play. My team was Stoke and so I jumped on the band-
wagon. Now, many years later, all those adolescent loyalties had
been long forgotten. As a professional, I am able to play for any
team, providing the financial remuneration and the stature of the
club are adequate for my requirements. This approach, which is
taken by nearly all professionals, may seem mercenary to those
supporters who view the game through misty eyes. However, having said this, affection and loyalty towards a club can follow after
a successful and productive liaison.

My first game for Leeds was away at Blackburn Rovers. It was
very much a fresh start for me. I was at a new club in a different
division, and it was my first game of the nineties. My debut could
not have gone better as I scored in a 2–1 victory, although the
result would have been different had Blackburn converted a last-
minute penalty.

It is always difficult moving to a new club, but my transfer was
made easier by the fact that there were familiar faces already at
Leeds. Besides the manager, coach Mick Hennigan, Mel Sterland,
Carl Shutt, Glynn Snodin, John Pearson and Dylan Kerr had all
been with me at Sheffield Wednesday. It was particularly pleasing
to link up with Mel, who had always been a great provider of
crosses for me.

It had worked with Howard Wilkinson for four successful years
at Wednesday and, in my second spell it was interesting to note the
contrast in style. It was soon apparent that he had retained the
principles of thorough preparation of his teams, both tactically
and physically. What was also noticeable was his more relaxed
attitude towards his job. He had never been one to delegate, but
now he was doing just that. Coach Mick Hennigan was allowed to
take training and so give Wilkinson, himself and the players a vital
break from each other.

The infamous cross-country runs on a Monday or Tuesday, legendary throughout English football, had been omitted from the
Leeds training schedule, and I, for one, was not complaining. At

Wednesday, the set-piece rehearsals had been so prolonged that they had become tests of endurance. We had also been required to show the same level of commitment as we would in a match situation. Now at Leeds, although great importance was still put upon these set-piece practices, their length and severity had been greatly reduced.

Financial restrictions at the manager's previous club had necessitated a more direct style of football. The Leeds team in his first full season in charge, 1989-90, had still retained this direct approach, but I sensed a subtle change. It was a change that was to be a dramatic one eighteen months later. The extra spending power had enabled the manager to acquire players who could play a more sophisticated type of football. His first such signing was Gordon Strachan. Gordon was signed from Manchester United, where the last part of his stay had been relatively unproductive. At Elland Road he had experienced something of a renaissance and was playing arguably the best football of his career. He was to be a guiding light throughout the whole of that Second Division campaign.

Much has been made of Gordon's diet of porridge and bananas (not forgetting the seaweed pills). The press has seized upon this, declaring it to be the reason for the longevity of his career. In fact, all that Gordon was doing was following the high-carbohydrate diet that has proved to be so beneficial in enhancing his performance. He also used the principles of biokinetics as an aid to performance. Biokinetics involves the massage of the energy points around the body to enable the energy flow to be at a maximum during a game. Norwegian Harold Oyen, a lecturer in biokinetics, had introduced this technique to Gordon some time before. Gordon used his strength of character to prove that there can be life after thirty for footballers who still retain their enthusiasm and desire.

Gordon's diminutive stature was always going to prevent him from being the bravest of players physically, but this did not stop him from showing a different type of bravery that is not often appreciated outside the game but is equally important – accepting possession of the ball in tight situations. It is a responsibility that few players relish.

My second game in Leeds colours was against my first club, Stoke City. It was sad to see them languishing at the bottom of the Second Division, with relegation to the Third seeming inevitable.

Once the rot sets into a club, it is difficult to stop. The deterioration process was evident during the time I was with Stoke, and so the position they were now in was hardly a shock. Such is the turnover of players and staff at clubs, it was surprising to see two familiar faces from my days in the Potteries – goalkeeper Peter Fox, and the coach, Tony Lacey, who was still in charge of the youth squad. Our 2–0 victory pushed my old club closer to the brink; they duly finished last.

Although I was playing in an unfamiliar division, many of the clubs we were to play against had been in the First Division at some stage of my career. Some had a chance to return to their former status, while others were obviously in decline.

I soon became aware of the criticism the manager was receiving in certain sections of the press about Leeds' style of play. He had been labelled as an exponent of the long-ball game during his spell at Sheffield Wednesday. This description of him was certainly justifiable for the first two years of Wednesday's return to the First Division. After that he had tried to introduce a more cultured game, but was severely hampered by the lack of funds needed to purchase players of the requisite quality.

When he joined Leeds in October 1988, the team were in twenty-third place in the Second Division and relegation to the Third was a distinct possibility. The long-ball game enables a manager to transform a team of limited ability into an effective one. The manager was also aware that these tactics were the most immediate method of getting a team into the First Division. With this in mind, a direct style was adopted, enabling the club to escape relegation and consolidate its position in the Second Division.

When I arrived in January 1990, it was clear that this style had been modified slightly to utilise players such as Gordon Strachan. This aspect had gone unnoticed, overshadowed to some extent by the surprise purchase of Vinnie Jones from Wimbledon. This signing seemed only to confirm the manager's commitment to the long-ball game – Wimbledon had been the most notorious users of this system for some time and Vinnie, in many ways, epitomised all that the team had stood for.

It seems that the manager bought Vinnie for two reasons; one was his knowledge of playing the direct game and the second was his reputation both on and off the field. He had been tagged a hard man by the press, who were quick to see an opportunity to create a national figure out of Vinnie. He had gone along with all the publicity to such an extent that he had become a cult figure. With his outrageous haircut and his larger-than-life personality, he had become a focal point in motivating the long-suffering Leeds supporters.

His hard-man image on the field was something that had been greatly exaggerated. Vinnie seemed more concerned about improving his game while he was at Leeds than intimidating the opposition. There is no doubt that he did develop during his stay at Elland Road and he left a better player for it. In the dressing room, he was a bubbly, outgoing character who was great for morale. Each day he would turn up for training in a different tracksuit. It seemed he had a different one for each day of the year. He enjoyed his celebrity status to the full. Some people found his unabashed desire for publicity a little hard to accept. This was not a problem for me and we got on very well – everyone to their own, and after all, only a few years previously he had seemed to be destined to spend the rest of his life on a building site.

As the season neared its conclusion, the pressure to maintain our position as leaders intensified. It was eventually to reach a level that was far greater than that of our title-winning campaign. Edginess had already crept into our play when, in my eighth game, we met Port Vale at home. It was strange to be playing against my father's old team after watching them so many years before as a child. Back then, they had been a struggling Fourth Division outfit with no prospects of changing their predicament. On the night, they performed well and were unfortunate only to come away with a 0–0 scoreline. We had now gone four games without a win and our next match at Oxford was going to be vital.

There was no doubt that the jitters had set in – the game started disastrously and we were soon 2–0 down. Our promotion dreams seemed to be falling apart around us. We then proceeded to stage a gritty fightback that enabled us to win the match 4–2. It was one of the most significant results of our campaign. Defeat in this game could have been followed by many more.

During the dying minutes of the match we were awarded a penalty. We were well on top, two goals ahead, and as I had scored twice, I grabbed the ball in an attempt to get a hat trick. I struck the spot kick well, but, unfortunately, directed it straight at the Oxford keeper, who could not avoid saving it. The final whistle blew and I walked off the pitch, disappointed at not getting my hat trick, but still happy with our victory and my two goals. The manager did not share my feelings. On entering our dressing room, I received a verbal lashing for taking the penalty. Our regular taker, Gordon Strachan, was also rebuked for allowing me to take it. The manager was greatly concerned about goal difference being a deciding factor in our quest for promotion and the championship – he had once seen Chelsea take the Second Division title on goal difference from Wednesday during his time at Hillsborough. My miss might yet prove vital.

That victory set us up for a run of three consecutive wins, which allowed us to put a bit of distance between ourselves and Sheffield United, our closest rivals. Then a run of four games without a victory enabled United to close the gap once more.

Our next match was against United at Elland Road, in front of the highest Second Division crowd of the season. Nearly 33,000 people saw us rise to the occasion and finish comfortable 4–0 winners. It seemed now, with only four games to play, that we would surely gain promotion and finish as champions.

A disappointing draw away to Brighton was shrugged off. Our next game was at home to Barnsley, who were hovering one place from the relegation zone; surely there would be no slip-ups here. Our football that evening, though, was filled with tension. Home matches were becoming more of an ordeal than away games. The supporters were so desperate for us to gain promotion, that their frustration was almost tangible on the pitch. The unthinkable happened, and Barnsley won 2–1. All the investment and effort that had been injected throughout the season seemed to be evaporating into nothing.

There was no time to rectify our poor performance on the training field. Three days later, we were again playing at home, this time to Leicester City in our penultimate fixture. It was a game that we simply had to win. Sheffield United and now Newcastle United were only a win from overtaking us. Not only was the championship at risk, but promotion too.

With five minutes to go, the score remained at 1–1. Mel Sterland had fired us ahead, only for Gary McAllister to equalise for Leicester with a tremendous strike. It was ironic that his goal could have cost us promotion, and thus his £1 million move to Leeds a few weeks later might not have taken place. With time fast running out, the tension was unbearable. The Leeds team appeared to be full of players with tired legs and weary minds as we desperately tried to conjure up a winning goal. Just when it seemed that a draw was inevitable, up popped Gordon Strachan with a marvellous first-time shot from the edge of the box. The ball ripped into the back of the net, causing the whole ground to erupt. The sense of relief felt by players and supporters alike was as great as I have ever experienced. Gordon's goal was as important as any he had scored in his life.

Victory against Leicester had been vital, with both our rivals having won their respective matches. The race for promotion would now go to the final Saturday, although we were still in prime position. A win in our final match at Bournemouth would guarantee us the championship; anything less could result in a place in the play-offs.

As we travelled down to Bournemouth, the feeling was similar to that of a Cup Final. In many ways it was that important – our whole season would be decided in one match. It was a bank holiday weekend and it seemed that the whole of Leeds had travelled down with us. The scenes around the ground were chaotic. There were so many Leeds supporters outside the stadium that the coach was unable to reach the main entrance. We were dropped off on the opposite side and entered the ground through a back entrance. It was obvious that many fans did not have tickets. Many were trying to get into the ground through adjacent gardens, while others even tried to sneak in with the team. When we got into the stadium, some youths had already gained illegal entry and were being ejected by the police. The venue was ludicrously ill-equipped for a game of this importance. The problem was exacerbated by the Football League's decision to play the fixture on a bank holiday weekend. It had encouraged even more people to make the long journey from Yorkshire.

When the game finally kicked off, the resulting football hardly befitted the occasion. A bone-hard pitch, high temperatures and the tremendous tension all combined to produce a very poor match. At half-time, although we had created two good chances, the scoreline was goalless. The news filtering through to our dressing room was that our rivals were ahead in their games.

Shortly after the restart, Chris Kamara sent over a superbly driven cross, which met full-on with my head. The power of the cross was such that the resulting header flew over the Bournemouth keeper's head and into the goal before he had time to react. We hung on desperately to our lead until the final whistle eventually blew. We had at last become Second Division champions.

The jubilant scenes in the dressing room and on the journey home were overshadowed by news of the after-match rioting. Leeds had endured eight years of discredit, both on and off the field. Now, just when it seemed we had answered our critics on both fronts, some of our so-called supporters had let us down badly. All the success we had achieved on the pitch had now been devalued by actions off it. Those involved with the running of the club had also been done a great disservice. Great efforts had been made during the season to rid the club of the hooligan element which had been associated with Leeds for many years. There had been a total absence of trouble up until this point, and the mood at Elland Road had changed to such an extent that families had started to attend home matches once again. This had been encouraged by the creation of a 'family stand' and the introduction of a membership scheme which prohibited any supporter from buying a ticket unless he or she was a fully vetted member.

As a result of the disturbances at Bournemouth, Leeds were subsequently punished and were one more incident away from possible expulsion from the League. It was a harsh decision for a club that had done everything possible to deter such occurrences. Thankfully, that incident appears to have been a temporary blip. The days when it was fashionable to be a troublemaker at Elland Road are now long gone. Hooliganism was a social trend which enjoyed a prolonged life with some sections of the Leeds supporters. Largely through the club's efforts, these people have been made to see reason and are now attending matches purely for the football.

During the end-of-season trip to Mallorca, John Pearson, our reserve centre forward, suffered the ultimate humiliation. Although John had many admirable qualities as a footballer, speed was not one of them. He had endured merciless mickey-taking about his lack of pace for some considerable time, being taunted with jibes that even our cleaning ladies could beat him in a twenty-yard sprint.

After a few beers at a beachside bar, it was decided, by some of the more energetic members of our party, to hold a sprint competition on the beach. John, the eternal optimist, decided to enter, no doubt encouraged by the participation of Sean Hardy, our kit manager, and Alan Sutton, our physiotherapist who was in his mid-forties. Several last places later, John's only chance of victory came when he was paired against Alan Sutton, to decide who received the wooden spoon. It was no competition – our balding physiotherapist with the slight weight problem never gave him a chance.

The team's success had encouraged the board to make money available for new signings. During the close season, Gary Mc-Allister, John Lukic and Chris Whyte were signed for combined fees of nearly £3 million. The club's return to the First Division for the first time in eight years had excited the supporters as well. Record-breaking season-ticket sales were recorded and our first game in the First Division was eagerly awaited.

The season kicked off at Goodison Park, with a 3–2 victory over Everton. It was a marvellous result in our first game back, especially as it was a match that had been viewed with some trepidation. Even though I had been out of the First Division for only six months, I found the game an extremely tension-filled affair. Confidence is a fragile commodity with footballers and even this short absence had cast doubts into my mind.

Leeds had started the season with an exciting new-look midfield of Strachan, Batty, McAllister and Speed. Of the four, only Gordon Strachan and Gary McAllister had ever played in the First Division before, but nevertheless the quality of the quartet could not be doubted.

Gary Speed had come into the side during the latter part of the previous season, and had showed great potential. It was enough to earn him his first Welsh cap during the summer and he started the new campaign oozing with confidence. Gary seems to have everything going for him; he's strong, good in the air and is a tremendous striker of the ball. To make things worse, he has the kind of film-star good looks that have the girls falling at his feet.

His closest friend at the club just happened to be his midfield partner, David Batty. It was rumoured they were as devastating with the girls off the pitch as they were with the ball on it. It was something I could easily believe. David's tenacity in the tackle and his distribution of the ball were soon to be recognised by England. His non-stop style of play is a true reflection of his personality. He must have been a hyperactive child who never calmed down, for I do not think I have seen him still for more than five minutes at a time. His boredom threshold is so low that during the sometimes arduous set-piece rehearsals, the manager sends him to a quiet corner of the training ground, so he can entertain himself with his favourite pastime of drilling balls into a goal. David has such a powerful and accurate strike in training that I find it difficult to understand why he is not a more regular goalscorer in matches.

Gary McAllister's introduction brought a more subtle cutting edge to the Leeds midfield. His vision, delicate touch and strong off-the-ball running added an extra dimension to the team. He also possesses a powerful shot that is capable of getting his goalscoring tally into double figures. He settled in well during his first season with the club, but then fully blossomed in his second and in doing so established himself as a Scotland regular.

Gary's arrival forced Vinnie Jones out of the side. Vinnie had done a good job during our Second Division campaign, but that alone could not guarantee him a place in the First Division. Football is a ruthless business, especially at the top. If a manager thinks he can replace a player with a better one, then he will. There can be no room for misguided loyalties if a team is to become the best.

The manager had made his decision and Vinnie had taken it well in the circumstances. It had obviously hit him hard, but he did not allow it to affect his general demeanour in and around the ground. One day after training he burst into the manager's office with a double-barrelled shotgun in his hand (Vinnie was a keen shot and was off to a shoot directly after training). He jokingly pointed the gun at the surprised manager and threatened him with both barrels if he did not get his place back! It seemed to do the trick. Vinnie returned for our fourth match of the season at Luton. The game finished in a 1–0 defeat and a few days later Vinnie was transferred to Sheffield United, where he would link up again with his former Wimbledon manager, Dave Bassett.

After a bright start to the season, our form slipped. We then began a fourteen-match unbeaten run which saw us rise from eleventh to third in the table. The first match in this run was away to Aston Villa. It was a game that saw Chris Kamara make his full First Division debut, after seventeen years of hard slog in the lower divisions. It was great to see Chris make it after all the hard work he had put in over the years. At thirty-three, there could not have been a fitter or more enthusiastic professional in the League, and if anyone had earned the right to play in the First Division, it was him.

The following game marked the start of a sequence in which I scored in six consecutive games. A bookmaker's stall for

Ladbrokes had recently been installed at the ground. Although I was not a gambler I had successfully backed myself to score the opening goal in several of these matches. Unfortunately, after I'd made a tidy sum, the news leaked to the press. Ladbrokes decided that backing myself might be construed to be suspicious and a ban was imposed throughout the whole of the Ladbrokes chain on any player placing bets on himself. It seemed to be an overreaction to the situation – the bets were, after all, positive ones, and hardly involved earth-shattering sums of money.

Our impressive unbeaten run came to an abrupt end when we travelled to Anfield to play Liverpool. If we had had any delusions about winning the championship that season, they were soon ended by a crushing 3–0 defeat. We still had some way to go before we could compete with the best and beat them. Not only did we lack the quality to overcome Liverpool, but we were extremely naive in going for their throats straight from the kick-off. It had been a valuable lesson for us.

Just over three weeks later we played Arsenal in the fourth round of the FA Cup. We knew that Arsenal and Liverpool were the two teams that we had to emulate and then surpass. They, above all others, had set the standards of recent seasons. Our encounter with the Gunners would provide us with another valuable update on our progress.

The tie went to three replays but eventually Arsenal's quality overcame us. During the four matches there had not been a lot to choose between two very accomplished sides. In fact, in the second replay at Highbury, we should have killed the tie off. Instead our lack of belief and conviction in ourselves proved inhibitive. Both teams proved to be well organised and disciplined, but Arsenal had the edge when it came to those flashes of quality that are so essential for a team to be able to win the crucial matches. In essence, it was becoming increasingly obvious that we were two or three quality players away from being serious title contenders.

Sandwiched right in the middle of our FA Cup marathon was a League game against Tottenham Hotspur at White Hart Lane. It turned out to be one of the most traumatic matches of my career.

Two minutes after the kick-off, I chased after a ball by the touchline. I stooped to head it in an attempt to prevent it from going out of the field of play. As I lowered my head, Steve Sedgley, the Spurs centre half, attempted to clear the ball with his foot. His boot accidentally hit my jaw square-on and I was immediately rendered unconscious. My momentum carried me on to the cinder track surrounding the pitch where I fell face first into the ground. In my unconscious state, I had been unable to use my hands to break the fall, and had taken the brunt of my near-fourteen-stone frame full on my face.

My nose was broken in two places and the skin covering it had been wiped away to expose the bone. My two front teeth had torn through my upper lip, forcing one of the teeth to break in two, and my forehead, chin and left side of my face had suffered severe graze wounds.

As I was led from the track after being roused from my unconscious state, little did I know the extent of my injuries. All I could feel was a searing, burning pain emanating from my face. My mouth was full of grit and yet all I could taste was blood. I was taken to the accident unit of the local hospital, where I was eventually patched up. A nurse quietly told me I should seek the help of a plastic surgeon because of the missing areas of skin on my nose, and the substantial amount of grit still left in my wounds.

Mervyn Day, our stand-by goalkeeper, had accompanied me throughout my ordeal and had been a great comfort in the strange surroundings of the hospital. I remember turning to him and saying: 'Whatever I get paid, it isn't enough for this!' At the time I meant it.

The journey back on the team coach was the most painful I have ever made. I could see that the rest of the players were shocked by my condition. I was so bloodied and swollen that I looked as though I had been involved in a car accident. I can remember Gordon Strachan saying he had never seen anything like it.

I was transferred to a private hospital on my return to Leeds and was operated on the following morning. Andrew Bachelor, the plastic surgeon, had reopened and cleaned all my wounds. They were then restitched in such a way that scarring would be kept to a minimum. He had solved the problem of the missing skin on my nose by cutting an inverted V shape between my eyebrows and then pulling the skin on my forehead down to cover the missing area. Shortly after the operation I was shown my face in a mirror. It was hard to recognise my bloodied and swollen features. I looked so horrific that my two-year-old son, Joseph, was afraid to come near me!

Despite all of this I was already thinking about our Rumbelows

Cup semi-final against Manchester United, which was to be played a week later at Old Trafford. My decision to play in that game was made after consultation with a neurosurgeon, who gave me the all-clear. There had been no neurological damage, but I was aware that my facial wounds had barely had time to heal and were still some way from being strong enough to take the punishment of a competitive match. We visited the boxing trainer, Brendan Ingle, who had worked for many years with middleweight champion Herol 'Bomber' Graham. Brendan, who was one of the best 'cuts' men in the business, advised me to bathe my injuries with surgical spirit in order to harden the skin. For matches, I was to paint them with plastic skin, which is a resin-like fluid that sets hard when applied, to form a second skin.

So, eight days after the incident, I walked out at Old Trafford with around thirty stitches still in my wounds. I had daubed the plastic skin all over them, which made my appearance even more grisly. As the two teams lined up to go out, I glanced across at Bryan Robson, who was staring at me. The look on his face said it all. He obviously thought I was crazy to play, and with hindsight I realise that he was right. The decision to play had been left entirely to me. If it had not been such an important game, I probably would not have done so, but it was the kind of match that every professional dreams of playing in, and I could not bear the thought of missing out. I decided, after that game, never to make the same error again.

From January until the end of the season, we were to hold fourth place for all but two matches. With six games left we played Liverpool again, but this time at Elland Road. Once again we were confident, and once again it was misplaced. In a devastating opening twenty-eight minutes, when John Barnes took us apart almost single-handedly, we conceded four goals without reply. It was Liverpool at their very best. In the second half, however, they showed early signs of the problems they would have the following season. They allowed us to stage a rousing fightback and the game eventually finished 5–4 in their favour. Even though I left the field with the match ball after scoring a second-half hat trick, I still finished on the losing side. If it had not been for what I believed at the time to be a dubious refereeing decision, the match would have been drawn. I was adjudged to have fouled goalkeeper Mike Hooper when challenging for a cross. I met the ball first and headed it into the empty goal without making any contact with my opponent, but this did not stop the referee from blowing for a foul.

The incident highlighted just how overprotected goalkeepers have become. If a goalkeeper drops the ball or fails to reach it when being challenged, most referees today instinctively react by giving a free kick, regardless of whether an infringement has taken place. It seems it is almost impossible for a player to challenge a goalkeeper successfully. I do not advocate a return to the days when forwards could shoulder-charge a keeper, but I do think referees have gone too far in the opposite direction. The balance must be redressed and I do of course speak as an unbiased striker.

Despite my disallowed goal, this match took my tally to twenty-seven for the season. I had already passed my previous best total by four. My goalscoring achievements earned me a call-up to the England B team for the match against Iceland at Vicarage Road, Watford. I had given up all hope of any international recognition and although it was only the B team, it was still a pleasant surprise.

We met the night before the game at Luton, along with the full squad who were playing in midweek. It was nice to bump into my ex-Forest colleagues, Nigel Clough, Stuart Pearce, Steve Hodge and Des Walker, who were all with the senior party.

Both squads assembled together for dinner, but before we ate, manager Graham Taylor spoke to us all. To my amazement he started to criticise the previous England performance. I was even more surprised when he singled out captain Gary Lineker for a below-par performance in this game. It was a talk that seemed better suited to a more intimate environment. (A year later, he was still at it. After England's draw against Brazil, when Lineker missed a penalty, he remarked that it had been like playing with ten men – a comment that I know upset Gary.) The following morning we met to be told the team. I was chosen to play alongside Nigel Clough. My clubmate David Batty also played, alongside our future Leeds colleagues, Steve Hodge and Tony Dorigo. It was an attempt to recreate a Forest-style system.

The match was played on a rock-hard pitch in front of three thousand people, and it was predictable that the football on show was uninspired. Our attempt to play Forest's short passing game failed miserably. This was inevitable when you consider that four members of the team came from Wimbledon or Crystal Palace, clubs notorious for their long-ball approach. The end result was a disjointed performance from a side thrown together only a few hours before, and a drab 1–0 win.

My brief involvement with the England set-up made me realise what a difficult task any England manager faces. He is given just a few days with his players and in that time he must organise them into a winning outfit. In the English First Division there is a wide array of differing styles which makes the task even more difficult. On the Continent, countries like Germany, France and Italy each have an identifiable style which is common to all clubs. Therefore, players moving up to international level are required to play exactly as they do week in, week out for their club.

Graham Taylor was burdened with another problem. He had to refrain from being too critical or too personal about his squad. They were not his players and would go back to their respective clubs after their brief stay with him. The fact that he could not get inside their minds, as he could at club level, appeared to frustrate him.

Leeds' season finished at Nottingham Forest with a 4–3 defeat. Although the result was disappointing, my two goals in the game brought my tally for the season to thirty-one. I had broken the thirty mark for the first time in my career and the figure was enough for me to finish as the First Division's top scorer. It was a feat I had been trying to achieve for over a decade.

The two goals at Forest had also enabled me to emulate my late father, Roy, by passing the two-hundred-goal mark. All in all it had been quite a season – although nothing like as extraordinary, it transpired, as what was to follow.

· 9 ·

Thirtysomething and beyond

Amidst all the close-season transfer speculation that inevitably followed Leeds' championship success in 1992, I was amused to read in one tabloid newspaper of the club's alleged interest in a young striker 'to replace Lee Chapman, who is nearing the end'.

Reports of my retirement have been greatly exaggerated. In the blinkered eyes of many sections of the press, it seems that once a player passes the magic age of thirty, his days are suddenly numbered. They ignore the fact that if he is both dedicated and determined enough, he can play on well into his thirties, and still perform as he did many years earlier. Ray Wilkins, Peter Reid and my Leeds team-mate, Gordon Strachan, are just a few examples. Although I have come to expect this limited line of thought, it nevertheless brings a wry smile to my face, especially when my level of physical fitness has never been greater. It is ironic that such negative press should come during the period when I have been playing the finest football of my career and enjoying the most success.

This mentality is not just restricted to our country. After the 1991–92 season, I was talking to a well-known agent who informed me that my name had been mentioned by several top Italian clubs. They were genuinely interested until the moment my age was discussed. At this point, the conversations ended.

Inevitably my career, like everybody else's, will come to an end at some stage. When that time will be, I cannot say, but I would like to think I will decide for myself, and not have the decision made for me.

Retirement is a time nearly all footballers dread. Many put it to the back of their minds in the hope it may never happen, and as a result are totally unprepared for life after football. Most players have only ever known the world of football and are largely ill-equipped for a job outside it. Footballers do not need any academic qualifications and as a result many neglect their studies at school. They are committed to a career in football and never contemplate the possibility of failure.

For a player nearing the end of his career, a move into coaching or management seems a natural progression. These are precarious positions at the best of times and do not guarantee any long-term security. Those who attain such positions soon realise that life is very different on the other side of the fence.

Traditionally, for those leaving the game, the favourite alternatives have been to run a pub or open a sports shop. Players who go into the former business often do so with disastrous effects on their waistlines. I have always found it sad to see the once-lithe forms of my former idols bloated after years behind a bar. In recent times, many ex-footballers have become insurance salesmen. Footballers are usually very good socialisers and are therefore well suited to this line of work. If they are already instantly recognisable to their potential clients, selling a policy becomes that much easier.

The emergence of the agent in the past few years has opened up another avenue to ageing professionals. Players who have enjoyed successful careers have usually made many useful contacts along the way. Once again, their fame and notoriety are a great help in securing new clients – John Hollins, Frank McLintock and Liam Brady are just a few examples.

For the minority who entered football at a later stage in their lives, there is always the possibility of returning to their original line of work – Stuart Pearce (electrician) and Carl Shutt (mechanic) are two who came into the game with a trade behind them to which they could return if necessary. Of those who have chosen to move away from football, I am sure that nearly all miss the day-to-day involvement with a club. It must be a strange feeling to find yourself suddenly on your own after years of being cosseted in the womb-like environment that exists at most professional clubs. Although not all players enjoy the routine of training, most would miss the special blend of dressing-room banter that exists in football and the camaraderie that is created as a result of it. The most difficult thing to come to terms with would be the absence of a match day. This is the one thing all footballers relish; the focal point of their week. Even those who cannot be stimulated in training suddenly come to life shortly before a game.

Personally, I will greatly miss performing in front of crowds of thirty thousand plus. Furthermore, as a goalscoring striker, I have been fortunate enough for many years to experience the ultimate thrill in football. The buzz that I experience whenever I score has become extremely addictive. Like a junkie, it has become necessary for me to get my fixes on a regular basis. When I can no longer obtain them, I am bound to suffer withdrawal symptoms.

The one thing that no player will miss is the extensive travelling that all professionals have to endure. The endless hours spent on coaches and in hotels become more tedious as time goes by.

Looking back over my career, it is almost a case of 'Regrets, I've had a few, but then again too many to mention'. If I could have planned it there is no doubt I would have liked it to have gone far more smoothly than it has. After an encouraging, carefree start at Stoke City, I got my dream move, to Arsenal, and this was when things started to go wrong. They continued in the same vein when I made the misjudgement of signing for Sunderland. The Arsenal and Sunderland period was a two-year spell that inflicted almost irreparable damage on my career. In fact, I had reached such a low point that any further deterioration could have resulted in a slide down into the lower divisions and beyond.

When I moved to Sheffield Wednesday I consciously made the decision that I could not allow myself to remain in that state of mind for any longer, for the sake of my self-esteem. Throughout the whole experience, my saving grace was that I had retained a semblance of belief in my ability to succeed. I had also gained an inner strength that was to help me enormously in the following years. My dismal period in London and the north-east did teach me to appreciate fully the success I enjoyed in later years. When you have experienced such abject failure, any subsequent triumphs are all the more enjoyable.

After my rehabilitation period with Wednesday, I made another bad decision when I agreed to join Niort, the French team I knew nothing about. However, my subsequent move to Forest marked the beginning of the most successful phase in my career. I am something of a fatalist, and from that moment on, everything seemed to fall into place.

A successful fifteen months with Forest included two Wembley finals and two winner's medals in the Littlewoods and Simod Cups. This was followed by my years at Leeds which included a Second Division championship medal and the highlight of my career, a First Division championship medal. In an amazing period of just under four years, I have been fortunate enough to win every domestic honour in English football, apart from the FA Cup. I was even able to fulfil a long-standing ambition by becoming the top First Division goalscorer in the 1990-91 season.

Despite my recent good fortune, I realise that my playing days cannot go on forever. With this in mind I have been getting involved in various areas of journalism, which have proved to be a stimulating diversion from my normal footballing duties. Whether they will lead to anything long-standing after I have retired remains to be seen, but they have nevertheless provided me with valuable experience.

I first started to work with BBC Radio 5 in a monthly discussion programme about topical aspects of the game. I talked about major issues, such as the new Premier League, with Charlton chairman Roger Alwen, and the widely travelled manager Bobby Gould. This was a great opportunity to discuss in depth subjects that most of the popular press would not be interested in, and it led to ITV and BSkyB asking me to appear on their live match broadcasts as a studio analyst. It is a job that is not as easy as it appears, especially when you are required to criticise ex-colleagues and other people in the game. Nevertheless, if the occasion arises, you must be honest in your criticism, otherwise there is no point in agreeing to appear in such a capacity.

As a TV pundit you are only giving your views on the game and nothing else. Football is a game of opinions and this inevitably leads to people disagreeing with you. During one of ITV's *The Match* programmes, in which Nottingham Forest were at home to Arsenal, I awarded the man-of-the-match champagne to Paul Merson. When it was announced over the tannoy, my decision was greeted with howls of derision from the home crowd, and as I entered the Forest boardroom after the game, I was met with icy stares. Those at Forest thought that Des Walker should have been given the verdict instead.

Two weeks later, I returned to the City Ground with Leeds. I was amazed to open the match programme and find that Brian Clough's notes were dedicated entirely to a stinging attack on my decision not to give Des Walker the award. During the opening five minutes of the game, I suddenly heard that unmistakable Clough voice boom: 'Eh, Chapman, Des Walker should have got the man-of-the-match award!'

My television appearances led to *The Times* newspaper inviting me to write a series of articles on the Leeds-Manchester United trilogy of matches in the League, FA Cup and Rumbelows Cup. This was the first serious writing I had undertaken since my A level days at college, over fourteen years previously. Although I was not initially confident, once I got into my stride I thoroughly enjoyed the experience.

I later worked with the *Observer* and wrote a series of articles on the 1992 European championships. In one, I found myself criticising Graham Taylor, the England manager. Bang goes *my* England career. . . . I was even asked by the *Sun* to comment on the France-England rugby union international in Paris – my impressions of the crowd, in which both sets of supporters mingled happily, and of the game itself, in which the French forwards behaved like English football hooligans.

I think it is important to open as many doors as possible, so that you can give yourself the widest possible choice of a career after football. Even though I would not entirely rule out management – I have learned that you should never say 'never' – I think it is vitally important not to be totally dependent on football for a living.

My late father, Roy, was a case in point. Unable to get a job in the game after his second parting with Stafford Rangers, he became a rep for a sports-goods company. Having spent all his life in the world of football, he was now enduring the stressful existence of a motorway rep. His inability to adapt to life outside football was, I believe, the cause of his fatal heart attack at the age of forty-nine.

A conflict with the chairman is not the only way for a manager to lose his job. Any budding boss must carefully consider whom he selects as his number two. The appointment of an over-ambitious assistant manager may prove to be a suicidal move. A friend of mine moved into management with a lower division club and appointed as his assistant an unemployed coach who, at the time, was only too pleased to have a job. Within a year, he had started to undermine the manager's tenure of the job with discreet, and not so discreet, comments to the chairman. Their relationship developed to such an extent that the assistant manager became a regular dinner guest of the chairman. When the club experienced a poor run of results, the chairman, with no little encouragement from the assistant, duly sacked the manager and promoted his newly acquired confidant instead. Alas, this is not an uncommon tale in the cut-throat world of football management. That is why most managers will not appoint a potential threat as their number two.

During my long and varied career, I have played under many different managers, and I have learned something from all of them – even the poor ones.

There is no doubt that the successful managers have all been autocratic to varying degrees. They have also imposed the rigid codes of discipline which I believe are vital for any footballer to perform to his potential – if a player is to be disciplined on the field, he must learn to be the same off it.

The two most successful managers I have played under are Brian Clough and Howard Wilkinson. Although their styles of management differ greatly, they do have one thing in common – all of their players are fully aware of what is expected of them on the pitch. If they cannot live up to these expectations, their stay at the club is short-lived. In some of the teams I have played for, it has been blatantly obvious that many players do not fully understand what their jobs on the field entail. The manager, it seems, is hoping it will all fall into place on the day. It very rarely does and this type of approach is always a recipe for disaster.

With Clough and Wilkinson, there are no such 'grey' areas and – especially with Clough – little room for discussion either. They both have a very clear idea of how they want their teams to play, and how their players should operate within them. As a professional, this is all you can ask from a manager – the rest is up to you.

Wilkinson has always rigidly laid down the framework within which his team must play, but he does on occasions consult his players on minor issues within that structure. He has always been a man of strong convictions but he has also been flexible enough to evolve as a manager. If a certain method has not worked, he has not been impervious to new ideas which have eventually led to a fresh approach. He has always believed in the thorough preparation of his teams, both physically and mentally – no other teams are fitter or better rehearsed in set-piece plays, although the methods of preparation in these two areas have been adapted over the years.

As an example of the thoroughness which characterises Wilkinson, not only in terms of his management style, he took up golf, but unlike most people he would not venture on to the course until he had mastered the basics through vigorous and repetitive practice.

Clough, on the other hand, has stuck with his tried and trusted methods with little variation. The game has changed beyond all recognition during his time in management, and I believe that it is now essential for teams to be as physically fit as possible, and to be well versed in their set-piece plays, both defensive and attacking. Even though Clough has had success in recent times, I feel it would have been even greater had his teams spent more time on these two areas.

The two men do have another thing in common – motivation. Any individual needs this in order to be successful in their chosen career, and football managers are no different. I believe that the motivating force for both Clough and Wilkinson has come from their playing careers.

Wilkinson was, by his own admission, a very ordinary winger in the lower divisions with Brighton and Sheffield Wednesday. He drifted out of League football in his late twenties and was forced to pursue an alternative career in teaching. This seems to have instilled a determination in him to do better in the game later in life. His subsequent success as a manager has enabled him to rub shoulders with the game's elite in a way which he never did as a player.

Clough's playing career was tragically ended when, at the age of twenty-eight, he suffered a crippling knee injury while hurling himself around an opposition's goalmouth on Sunderland's behalf. He was a striker whose goals-per-game record was nothing short of phenomenal, and there is no doubt that he was cut off in his prime. This cruel end to his playing days seems to have left him with an overwhelming sense of unfulfilment which I believe has been the driving force throughout his managerial career. Despite all his success as a manager, this feeling does not appear to have left him. Underneath his larger-than-life image, I still think there is a great sadness that has remained with him all these years.

For any player to become a successful manager, he must have great strength of character. Football management is a precarious business at the best of times. One week the hero, the next week the villain. Victory and defeat have to be treated in exactly the same manner. Principles have to be adhered to in times of adversity and at the same time, the ever-changing state of football must also be taken into account. Above all else, any budding manager must be at the right club, with a decent chairman supporting him, if he is going to make any kind of a mark in the game. The odds are heavily stacked against any young manager who does not have the right combination behind him.

Several of the managers I have played for have failed to recognise their limitations. Whilst they have been excellent coaches, they have not been cut out for life at the helm. Only a disastrous spell as manager brings the reality home, although some, it seems, will never learn.

Of the current crop of players nearing the end of their careers, two stand out as having great managerial potential – Ray Wilkins of Queen's Park Rangers, and my own colleague, Gordon Strachan. Both have knowledge of the game at the highest level and both have the strength of personality to survive the many pitfalls they will undoubtedly encounter.

At some time in the future, when my career will inevitably draw to a close, I would like to think I could go out at the top in the way that Gary Lineker and Denis Law have done. While some might say that they could have played for a few more years, it is far better to be remembered at your peak, rather than when your powers were on the wane. How sad it is to see once great players winding down through the lower divisions, a shadow of their former selves. It is understandable that some cannot let go of a lifestyle they have enjoyed for the best part of twenty years. It may be that financial pressures are preventing them from doing so as well. Nevertheless, it is like the great boxer who has one fight too many – he is always remembered for that last disastrous bout.

The issue is probably more important to me than most. My game has always been based on bravery and commitment. Although many have said that I have greatly improved as an all-round player in recent years, I can never lose sight of this fact. I have always been greatly motivated by the highly charged atmosphere of life in the First Division, and I would be asking many questions of myself if I had to play regularly in front of crowds of two or three thousand!

At some time during the nineties, I will eventually call it a day. I will be finishing my playing career at a time when the English game is undergoing the biggest upheaval in its history. The formation of the Premier League has given football the chance to move forward into the twenty-first century with renewed optimism. It remains to be seen if the opportunity will be fully grasped. The FA's *Blueprint for the Future of Football* contained many admirable proposals, which, if implemented, would greatly benefit the game. It now seems that the tunnel vision of a number of those in charge of Premier League clubs will hold the new League back in exactly the same way that it did the old Football League – vested interests will still prevail. One of the most important proposals is to reduce the number of clubs in the Premier League from twenty-two to eighteen. It seems that those running the game have at last realised that our top footballers are playing too many matches.

The well-being of the game in this country is very much dependent on the performance of our national team. England's success in the 1990 World Cup demonstrated this point. The First Division enjoyed increased attendance levels, while the lower echelons experienced a knock-on effect.

England went into the 1992 European Championship with a severe handicap: our players had played significantly more matches than their Continental counterparts. Not only did they have to overcome their formidable opponents, but they also had to resist the mental and physical fatigue that our marathon football season inevitably inflicts. The results in Sweden – for England at least – were as depressing as they were predictable. Having said that, Scotland performed with great spirit, and some style, although they were also eliminated after the first phase. A reduction in domestic games would enable our national team to compete on equal terms, and allow players to work on the technical side of their game in training during the week. At the moment, players scarcely have time to recover from one match before they are required to play in another. It is no surprise that English football does not produce as many technically gifted players as our European rivals.

The proposed reduction to eighteen clubs may never come about. Although the number of teams will be reduced to twenty after the 1994 World Cup, no date has been set for a further decrease. Typically, the majority of club chairmen have voted against such a move. Those outside the 'Big Six' clubs – in which I include Leeds United – fear relegation from the lucrative environment of the Premier League and the loss of revenue that would entail.

Perhaps it is asking too much of those who are running the game to be anything but myopic in their outlook. It is time to appoint an independent supremo of Premier League clubs, or to establish an independent committee, so that decisions can be made that are free of vested interests and have only the long-term good of the game at heart. Unless this happens, I fear the present mentality will prevail for the foreseeable future.

The introduction of the Premier League has enabled its member clubs to generate greatly increased levels of revenue. The most significant change has come from the sale of television rights, which I believe have been genuinely undervalued for some considerable time. The agreement with BSkyB television has brought football into a new age of commercialism. Football has long been the nation's favourite sporting spectacle, a fact that has not been reflected in the fees that have been paid by television companies for its coverage. Those running the game have been partly to blame because of their inability to see television as an important part of the long-term success of the sport. Football cannot survive on revenue from spectators alone – those days have long gone. Television revenue is now regarded as vital to the game's future. It is also seen as being crucial in giving football the high-profile image it needs to bring in lucrative sponsorship deals.

The Premier League will create a highly competitive atmosphere, not just for its member clubs, but for those in the Football League as well. It will now be essential for clubs to be run on a sound financial basis, just like any other business in any other industry. Many chairmen of football clubs are successful businessmen who have a passion for the game. For some reason, these shrewd operators have treated their clubs in a very unbusinesslike manner. Mike Watterson, the ex-Derby chairman, summed it up aptly: 'When I was a director of Sheffield United for six months, the chairman told me normal business standards did not apply in football. It was the most stupid advice I ever had.' Chairmen will no longer be able to use their club as hobbyhorses. The days of clubs being run as though the normal laws of economics do not apply are at an end. The Premier League has merely acted as a catalyst in bringing the situation to a head.

This will inevitably lead to a reduction in the number of full-time professional clubs. Many lower-division clubs will have to operate on a part-time basis, in order to reduce their running costs to an acceptable level. This in turn will mean a decrease in the number of full-time professionals employed by such clubs. Many lower-division players are very poorly paid and a move to part-time employment would be financially more attractive. With a job outside the game, not only would they be better paid, but they would also be better equipped for life after football.

Regionalisation of the lower divisions will be another essential move in enabling clubs to reduce operating costs. This measure would have another important effect – it would create more local derbies, which in turn would stimulate an increase in attendances.

After living in the past for so long, football in this country has been forced to face reality. Those who look realistically to the future will flourish, while those who bury their heads in the sand will surely perish.

There has never been a better time for youngsters to enter the professional game. For those who eventually make it, the financial rewards have never been greater. Players' salaries saw a dramatic increase in the late eighties. Up until that point the remuneration for English players fell well short of that earned by their European equivalents from Italy, Spain, West Germany and France. We have now reached a point where our top clubs can match all but a few of the top Continentals. The advent of the Premier League can only encourage a further improvement in the size of players' wage packets. When I entered the professional ranks in 1978, the concept of a player being able to earn enough during his career so that he would never have to work again was not a realistic one. Today that dream has become a strong possibility for many of our top players.

In many ways I would love to start my career all over again, especially in the exciting times football is now experiencing. However, my time in the game has always been eventful and I have tasted the full range of emotions that arise from success and failure. In my remaining years as a player, I would like to create many more memories to add to the collection I already have. I am still excited about the game and what I might still achieve in it. Having won the last Football League championship it would be extremely satisfying to win the inaugural Premier League title.

I am going to enjoy whatever time I have left as a top-class player, but life thereafter holds no fears for me – it will, I am sure, be every bit as interesting.

Lee Chapman
A Player's Story ... in figures

	Games (subs in brackets)					Goals				
	League	League Cup	FA Cup	Euro	Simod ZDS etc	League	League Cup	FA Cup	Euro	Simod ZDS
Stoke City (1978–82)	95 (4)	5	3	0	0	34	3	1	0	0
Plymouth Argyle (1978, loan)	3 (1)	0	0	0	0	0	0	0	0	0
Arsenal (1982–83)	15 (8)	0 (2)	0 (1)	2	0	4	0	0	2	0
Sunderland (1983–84)	14 (1)	0	2	0	0	3	0	1	0	0
Sheffield Wednesday (1984–88)	147 (2)	17	17 (1)	0	2 (1)	63	6	10	0	0
Niort (1988)	–	–	–	–	–	–	–	–	–	–
Nottingham Forest (1988–90)	48	12	5	0	6	15	6	3	0	3
Leeds United (1990–)	97	12	7	0	4	49	8	3	0	3
	419 (16)	46 (2)	34 (2)	2	12 (1)	168	23	18	2	6

GRAND TOTALS   513 (21) games, 217 goals (up to and including end of 1991–92 season; French statistics not available)

Index

INDEX

Liverpool 5, 17, 19, 20-1, 58, 59, 67, 68, 74, 78, 91, 116-18, 119, 136, 138-9
Lloyd, Larry 119
London 56, 62, 143
Lorimer, Peter 16
Lukic, John 20, 66, 69, 134
Lurkers 115
Luton Town 11-12, 17, 115, 123, 135
Lyas, Graham 110
Lyons, Mick 78-9, 81, 84

McAllister, Gary 4, 13, 15, 16, 21-2, 131, 134-5
McClair, Brian 13
McClelland, John 4
McFarland, Roy 92
McGee, Bert 85
McGrath, John 53
McIlroy, Sammy 68
McKenzie, Duncan 17
McLintock, Frank 142
McManus, Eric 53
Madden, Lawrie 89-90
Maddock, John 53
Magaluf 40, 72
Mahoney, John 27
Mallorca 40, 73, 118, 133
Manchester City 5, 15, 16, 34, 38, 40, 45, 122
Manchester United 1, 2, 3, 4-6, 7, 8-9, 12-13, 14-15, 16-19, 22-3, 26, 52, 55, 58, 67, 74, 78, 83, 105, 107, 122, 128, 138, 145
Manchester University 34
Mansfield 25
Marwood, Brian 86, 89, 90
Marwood, Lesley 86
Match of the Day 59
Match, The 10, 21, 144
Matthews, Stanley 26, 45
Maurice, Pierre 95
Maxwell, Ian 101, 103, 105
Maxwell, Robert 92, 101-2, 104-6, 118
Megson, Gary 37, 84, 86-7, 121
Mercer, Joe 38
Merson, Paul 144
Middlesbrough 24, 37, 112-13

Miklosko, Ludek 14
Millwall 107
Mirror Group 102
Moscow 60
Moscow Spartak 60
MTV 120

Neill, Terry 53, 54, 55, 56, 61, 62, 68
Newcastle United 131
Newport County 71
Newsome, Jon 4, 20
Niagara Falls 86
Nicholas, Charlie 66, 67-8
Nîmes 10
Niort 10, 92, 94-106, 108, 114, 143
Norwich 14, 23, 59, 64, 67
Nottingham 117
Nottingham Forest 4, 17-19, 56, 78, 80, 90, 92, 93, 94, 99, 101-7, 108-25, 140, 143, 144
Notts County 10, 11, 40, 52
Nuneaton Borough 27

Observer 145
O'Callaghan, Brendan 42-3, 44
O'Kane, Liam 110, 112, 125
Oxford 105, 130-1
Oyen, Harold 128

Palin, Michael 25
Paish, Wilf 16
Pallister, Gary 1, 5, 9
Palma Nova 74
Panathinaikos 45
Pattaya 80
Pearce, Stuart 109, 110, 114-15, 122, 125, 139, 142
Pearson, John 78, 79, 127, 133-4
Pejic, Mike 29
Pemberton, John 21
People 53
Pisa 116
Plymouth Argyle 36, 37, 38, 78, 84, 126
Pointon, Neil 15

Port Vale 25, 26, 30, 34, 53, 130
Premier League 144, 148-9, 150, 151
Proctor, Mark 74, 89
Pye, Freddie 34

Queen's Park Rangers 8, 13, 16, 48, 113, 148

Radio 5 144
Reading 105
Reid, John 93
Reid, Peter 141
Revie, Don 3, 16, 29, 124, 126, 127
Rice, Brian 114
Ritchie, John 28
Roach, Denis 99, 103 105-6
Robson, Bryan 5, 17, 74, 138
Robson, Stewart 57
Rowell, Gary 84
Royle, Joe 6
Rumbelows Cup 2, 7, 8, 16, 137-8, 145

Savoy Hotel 91
Schmeichel, Peter 5, 9
Scotland 135, 149
Sedgley, Steve 136-7
Sheffield 76, 84, 106
Sheffield United 3, 19-21, 37, 106, 131, 135, 150
Sheffield Wednesday 2, 4, 7-8, 19, 37, 71, 74-91, 92, 94, 98, 111, 121, 126, 128, 129, 143, 147
Sheridan, John 121
Sherwood, Steve 37
Shilton, Peter 33, 45, 100-1
Shreeves, Peter 7
Shutt, Carl 8, 80, 81-2, 127, 142
Silkman, Barry 36
Silver, Leslie 126-7
Simod Cup 115, 117, 118, 143
Smith, Alan 83
Smith, Denis 29
Snodin, Glynn 80, 127
Southampton 3, 17, 44

155